Piggyback® Songs
in
Praise of Jesus

Compiled by
Jean Warren

Illustrated by Marion Hopping Ekberg
Chorded by Barbara Robinson

Totline® Publications
A Division of Frank Schaffer Publications, Inc.
Torrance, California

ACKNOWLEDGMENTS

Special thanks to all who submitted songs for this book. Because of space limitiations, we regret that we were unable to include the names of many people who sent in songs similar to the ones chosen.

Edited by Elizabeth S. McKinnon
Illustrated by Marion Hopping Ekberg
Cover Design by Larry Countryman
Chorded by Barbara Robinson

ISBN 0-911019-11-1

Printed in the United States of America
Published by: Totline® Publications.
Editorial Office: P.O. Box 2250
                              Everett, WA 98203
Business Office: 23740 Hawthorne Blvd.
                              Torrance, CA 90505

CONTENTS

SONGS ABOUT JESUS

SONGS ABOUT OLD FRIENDS

SONGS ABOUT CHRISTMAS

SONGS ABOUT EASTER

SONGS ABOUT LOVE

SONGS ABOUT FRIENDSHIP AND GOODNESS

CHURCH, SUNDAY SCHOOL AND BIBLE SONGS

PRAYER, PRAISE AND THANK-YOU SONGS

TITLE INDEX

SONGS ABOUT JESUS

MARY HAD A LITTLE BOY

Sung to: "Mary Had a Little Lamb"

F
Mary had a little boy,

C7   F
Little boy, little boy.

F
Mary had a little boy,

    C7   F
And Jesus was His name.

F
Jesus grew to be a man,

C7   F
Be a man, be a man.

F
Jesus grew to be a man

     C7   F
And taught us right from wrong.

F
Jesus went to heal the sick,

C7   F
Heal the sick, heal the sick.

F
Jesus went to heal the sick,

  C7   F
Because he loved them so.

F
Jesus gave His life for us,

C7   F
Life for us, life for us.

F
Jesus gave His life for us.

C7   F
On the cross He died.

    F
On Easter Jesus rose again,

C7   F
Rose again, rose again.

    F
On Easter Jesus rose again.

    C7   F
He lives with God in heaven.

Cindy Dingwall
Palatine, IL

JESUS WAS A TINY BABY

Sung to: "Ten Little Indians"

C
Jesus was a tiny baby,

G7
Jesus was a tiny baby,

C
Jesus was a tiny baby,

G7   C
Born in Bethlehem.

C
Jesus grew to help the people,

G7
Jesus grew to help the people,

C
Jesus grew to help the people

G7   C
Learn about God's love.

C
Jesus cared for all in need,

G7
Jesus cared for all in need,

C
Jesus cared for all in need,

G7   C
And He loved them so.

Additional verse: "I am one of His disciples — I believe in Jesus."

Sue Schliecker
Waukesha, WI

LORD AND KING

Sung to: "Mary Had a Little Lamb"

F
Mary had a baby boy,

C7   F
Baby boy, baby boy.

F
Mary had a baby boy.

C7   F
Jesus was His name.

F
He was born in Bethlehem,

C7   F
Bethlehem, Bethlehem.

F
He was born in Bethlehem,

C7   F
Many years ago.

F
Jesus grew and began to teach,

C7   F
Began to teach, began to teach.

F
Jesus grew and began to teach

C7   F
All about God's love.

F
Jesus gave His life for us,

C7   F
Life for us, life for us.

F
Jesus gave His life for us

C7   F
So that we might live.

F
Jesus Christ is Lord and King,

C7   F
Lord and King, Lord and King.

F
Jesus Christ is Lord and King,

C7   F
Now and for ever.

Jan Ebmeier
Hutchinson, KS

MARY HAD A LITTLE BABE

Sung to: "Mary Had a Little Lamb"

F
Mary had a little babe,

C7   F
Little babe, little babe.

F
Mary had a little babe,

C7   F
Born in Bethlehem.

F
Jesus was the baby's name,

C7   F
Baby's name, baby's name.

F
Jesus was the baby's name,

C7   F
Born the King of kings.

F
Jesus died on Calvary,

C7   F
Calvary, Calvary.

F
Jesus died on Calvary

C7   F
And rose in victory.

Karen Brown
Bentonville, AR

JESUS WAS BORN

Sung to: "Skip to My Lou"

F
Jesus, Jesus, Jesus was born,

C7
Jesus, Jesus, Jesus was born,

F
Jesus, Jesus, Jesus was born,

C7   F
Born in Bethlehem.

Joyce Raymond
Des Moines, IA

JESUS GREW AS GOD HAD PLANNED

Sung to: "Michael, Row the Boat Ashore"

C   F C
Jesus grew as God had planned, Al-le-lu-ia.
Em   G   C G7C
Jesus grew as God had planned, Al-le-lu-ia.

C   F C
Jesus taught about God's love, Al-le-lu-ia.
Em   G   C G7C
Jesus taught about God's love, Al-le-lu-ia.

C   F C
Jesus prayed for everyone, Al-le-lu-ia.
Em   G   C G7C
Jesus prayed for everyone, Al-le-lu-ia.

C   F C
Jesus helped all those in need, Al-le-lu-ia.
Em   G   C G7C
Jesus helped all those in need, Al-le-lu-ia.

Bonnie Woodard
Louisville, KY

JESUS WAS THE SON OF GOD

Sung to: "The Mulberry Bush"

C
Jesus was the Son of God,
G7
Son of God, Son of God.
C
Jesus was the Son of God,
G7   C
Born in Bethlehem.

Karen Brown
Bentonville, AR

IN GOD'S WORD

Sung to: "Mary Had a Little Lamb"

F
Jesus taught us how to grow,
C7   F
How to grow, how to grow.
F
Jesus taught us how to grow.
  C7   F
It tells us in God's Word.

F
Jesus grew up strong and tall,
C7   F
Strong and tall, strong and tall.
F
Jesus grew up strong and tall.
  C7   F
It tells us in God's Word.

F
Jesus used His mind to learn,
C7   F
Mind to learn, mind to learn.
F
Jesus used His mind to learn.
  C7   F
It tells us in God's Word.

F
Jesus pleased our God above,
C7   F
God above, God above.
F
Jesus pleased our God above.
  C7   F
It tells us in God's Word.

F
Jesus learned to care and love,
C7   F
Care and love, care and love.
F
Jesus learned to care and love.
  C7   F
It tells us in God's Word.

Vicki L. Gilliam
Marlin, TX

JESUS

Sung to: "Bingo"

      C   F   C
There was a man who was God's Son,
  C   G7   C
And Jesus was His name-o.
C   F   G7 C   F
J-E-S-U-S, J-E-S-U-S, J-E-S-U-S,
    G7   C
And Jesus was His name-o.

         C   F   C
There was a man who loved children,
  C   G7   C
And Jesus was His name-o.
C   F   G7 C   F
J-E-S-U-S, J-E-S-U-S, J-E-S-U-S,
    G7   C
And Jesus was His name-o.

         C   F   C
There was a man who helped the poor,
  C   G7   C
And Jesus was His name-o.
C   F   G7 C   F
J-E-S-U-S, J-E-S-U-S, J-E-S-U-S,
    G7   C
And Jesus was His name-o.

         C   F   C
There was a man who healed the sick,
  C   G7   C
And Jesus was His name-o.
C   F   G7 C   F
J-E-S-U-S, J-E-S-U-S, J-E-S-U-S,
    G7   C
And Jesus was His name-o.

Additional verse: "There was a man who gave His life."

Maxine E. Pincott
Windsor, CT

GOD'S GIFT

Sung to: "Mary Had a Little Lamb"

F
Jesus was God's gift,
C7   F
God's gift, God's gift.
F
Jesus was God's gift,
C7   F
Sent for you and me.

Joey Gutierrez
Olympia, WA

JESUS WAS GOD'S SON

Sung to: "London Bridge"

F
Jesus was God's Son,
C7   F
God's Son, God's Son.
F
Jesus was God's Son,
C7   F
God's only Son.

Joyce Raymond
Des Moines, IA

TO SHOW HE WAS GOD'S SON

Sung to: "The Mulberry Bush"

C
Why did Jesus feed the crowd,
   (Pretend to eat.)
G7
Feed the crowd, feed the crowd?
C
Why did Jesus feed the crowd,
      G7   C
One day in Galilee?

Chorus:
   C
To show He was God's only Son,
G7
Only Son, only Son.
   C
To show He was God's only Son,
      G7   C
For all the world to see.

C
Why did Jesus heal the deaf,
   (Put hands over ears.)
G7
Heal the deaf, heal the deaf?
C
Why did Jesus heal the deaf,
      G7   C
One day in Galilee?

Chorus

Additional verses: "Why did Jesus stop the storm? Why did
Jesus heal the boy?" Have children march in a circle while
singing the verses, then stop and clap as they sing the chorus.

Author Unknown
Submitted by: Linda Schueler
Kandiyohi, MN

THIS IS THE BOAT

Sung to: "Yankee Doodle"

         C   G7
This is the boat where Jesus stood
   (Cup hands.)
         C   G
So everyone could hear Him.
         C   F
This is the house where Jesus sat
   (Put fists together.)
G7   C
So people could be near Him.
         C   G7
This is the mountain that He climbed,
   (Put fingertips together.)
         C   C G7
Where people heard Him teach.
C   F
Here's the temple where He went
   (Put knuckles together, pointer fingers up.)
G7   C
To worship and to preach.

Karen Vollmer
Wauseon, OH

LET THE CHILDREN COME TO ME

Sung to: "Mary Had a Little Lamb"

F
"Let the children come to me,
C7   F
Come to me, come to me.
F
Let the children come to me,"
C7   F
Jesus said one day.

F
Jesus told them of God's love,
C7   F
Of God's love, of God's love.
F
Jesus told them of God's love.
   C7   F
He came to light the way.

Jill Behnke
Hastings, MN

HE'S OUR SAVIOR

Sung to: "London Bridge"

C
Jesus made the blind to see,
G7   C
Blind to see, blind to see.
C
Jesus made the blind to see.
G7   C
He's our Savior.

C
Jesus made the lame to walk,
G7   C
Lame to walk, lame to walk.
C
Jesus made the lame to walk.
G7   C
He's our Savior.

C
Jesus made the deaf to hear,
G7   C
Deaf to hear, deaf to hear.
C
Jesus made the deaf to hear.
G7   C
He's our Savior.

Florence Dieckmann
Roanoke, VA

BE KIND LIKE JESUS

Sung to: "Twinkle, Twinkle, Little Star"

C   F   C
Jesus multiplied the bread
F   C   G7   C
So five thousand could be fed.
C   F   C   G7
He was kind and did good deeds,
C   F   C   G7
Helped the people in their need.
C   F   C
We should be like Jesus, too,
F   C   G7   C
Kind and helpful in all we do.

Karen Leslie
Erie, PA

JESUS ALWAYS HEALS THE SICK

Sung to: "The Mulberry Bush"

C
Jesus always heals the sick,
G7
Heals the sick, heals the sick.
C
Jesus always heals the sick.
G7   C
He helps everyone.

C
Jesus always calls the children,
G7
Calls the children, calls the children.
C
Jesus always calls the children,
G7   C
"Come unto me."

C
Jesus always loves us all,
G7
Loves us all, loves us all.
C
Jesus always loves us all.
G7   C
We are His special ones.

Karen Vollmer
Wauseon, OH

JESUS LOVED THE LITTLE CHILDREN

Sung to: "Ten Little Indians"

C
Jesus loved the little children,
G
All the big and little children.
C
Jesus loved the little children.
  G   C
He said, "Come to me."

Betty Silkunas
Philadelphia, PA

13

THE LOST SHEEP

Sung to: "The Mulberry Bush"

C
One wooly sheep went wandering,

G7
Wandering, wandering.

C
One wooly sheep went wandering,

G7   C
Away from the Shepherd and flock.

C
Then he fell down and was lost all alone,

G7
Lost all alone, lost all alone.

C
Then he fell down and was lost all alone,

G7   C
While the others stayed up on the hill.

    C
The Shepherd was sad and looked for His sheep,

G7
Looked for His sheep, looked for His sheep.

    C
The Shepherd was sad and looked for His sheep.

   G7   C
He looked for a very long time.

    C
He climbed up and down over boulders and rocks,

G7
Boulders and rocks, boulders and rocks.

    C
He climbed up and down over boulders and rocks,

G7   C
Until the sheep He did find.

    C
He lifted him up and carried him home,

G7
Carried him home, carried him home.

    C
He lifted him up and carried him home,

G7   C
All the way home on His shoulders.

Lois Poppe
Lincoln, NE

THE SHEPHERD'S SONG

Sung to: "London Bridge"

F
Have you seen my little lost sheep,

C7   F
Little lost sheep, little lost sheep?

F
Have you seen my little lost sheep?

   C7   F
I'll search until he's found.

F
When he's found I'll bring him home,

C7   F
Bring him home, bring him home.

F
When he's found I'll bring him home.

   C7   F
I love my little sheep so.

Vicki Claybrook
Kennewick, WA

14

SONGS ABOUT OLD FRIENDS

THEY FOLLOWED JESUS

Sung to: "Mary Had a Little Lamb"

F
Andrew brought his brother Simon,

C7   F
Brother Simon, brother Simon.

F
Andrew brought his brother Simon,

C7   F
And they followed Jesus.

F
Jesus changed his name to Peter,

C7   F
Name to Peter, name to Peter.

F
Jesus changed his name to Peter,

C7   F
And he followed Jesus.

F
Philip brought his friend Nathaniel,

C7   F
Friend Nathaniel, friend Nathaniel.

F
Philip brought his friend Nathaniel,

C7   F
And they followed Jesus.

                    Kathy Crawford
                    Hodgenville, KY

MATTHEW, MARK, LUKE AND JOHN

Sung to: "London Bridge"

F
Matthew, Mark, Luke and John

C7   F
Shared good news of our Christ,

F
Telling of His life on earth,

C7   F
In the gospel.

F
Telling of His birth and death,

C7   F
Friends and deeds, in their books,

F
Sharing all His works of love,

C7   F
In the gospel.

                    Marlene V. Filsinger
                    Snyder, NY

FISHING IN THE SEA

Sung to: "Skip to My Lou"

F
Peter and Andrew fishing in the sea,

C7
Peter and Andrew fishing in the sea,

F
Peter and Andrew fishing in the sea,

C7   F
Catching no fish for Jesus.

F
Jesus said, "Come, follow me."

C7
Jesus said, "Come, follow me.

F
Fishers of men, that's what you'll be."

C7   F
Catching them all for Jesus.

                    Judy Hall
                    Wytheville, VA

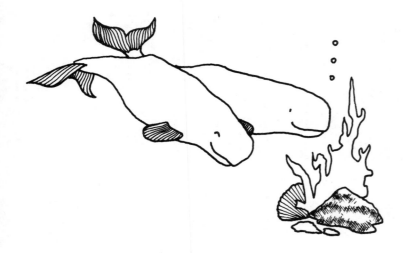

CALLING OF MATTHEW

Sung to: "Rock-A-Bye Baby"

G   D7
Jesus loved Peter, Jesus loved John.
                            G
Jesus loved James and Andrew, each one!
                                        D7
Could He love Matthew, who was so bad?
    G   C   D7   G
Yes! Jesus loves all, and that makes us glad!

Leah M. Serck
Seward, NE

PETER

Sung to: "Twinkle, Twinkle, Little Star"

C   F   C
Peter was a fisherman,
F   C   G7   C
By the Sea of Galilee.
C   F   C   G7
Not one fish had yet he caught,
C   F   C   G7
Empty nets then made him sad.
C   F   C
Jesus came and showed him how
G7   C   G7   C
To be a fisher of mankind.

Marlene V. Filsinger
Snyder, NY

TWELVE MEN PREACH OF HEAVEN

Sung to: "Row, Row, Row Your Boat"

C
One, two, three and four,
C
Five and six and seven,
C
Eight, nine, ten, eleven,
G7   C
Twelve men preach of heaven.

C
Jesus called each one,
C
For others they would care.
C
They were all His special friends,
    G7   C
The gospel they would share.

Sandy Gogel
Costa Mesa, CA

THE TWELVE DISCIPLES

Sung to: "This Old Man"

C
Jesus said, "Follow me,
F
Twelve disciples you will be."
C
James and John and Andrew, too,
G7   C
Philip and Bartholomew;
C
Thomas, James, Simon, eight,
F   G7
Judas, Matthew, don't be late,
C
Simon Peter, Thaddaeus, too —
G7   C
Twelve disciples, all for you.

Judy Hall
Wytheville, VA

JESUS STILLS THE STORM

Sung to: "Row, Row, Row Your Boat"

C
Jesus fell asleep

C
While they were afloat.

C
Then a wind blew very strong,

    G7   C
And water filled the boat.

C
"Help! Help!" His friends all cried,

C
"Whatever shall we do?"

C
"Just have faith," their Master said.

   G7   C
Away the big storm blew!

                     Bonnie Britton
               North Fort Meyers, FL

ONCE THERE WERE SOME FISHERMEN

Sung to: "Row, Row, Row Your Boat"

C
Once some fishermen

      C
Were on a stormy sea.

      C
They had no faith and so each cried,

G7   C
"Help, save me!"

C
Jesus came to them

      C
And said, "Why do you fear?

C
God is greater than a wave.

G7   C
Pray and He will hear."

              Marlene V. Filsinger
                  Snyder, NY

THE BLIND MEN

Sung to: "Eensy, Weensy Spider"

C
Once there were two blind men

     G7   C
Who couldn't see at all.

    C
Along came Jesus

     G7   C
Who listened to their call.

C
"Lord, have mercy,

G7   C
We would like to see."

    C
So Jesus touched and healed them,

   G7   C
And then the blind could see.

               Rachel Kramer
                 Beulah, ND

THE RAISING OF JAIRUS' DAUGHTER

Sung to: "The Farmer in the Dell"

F
Her father loved her so,
F
Her father loved her so.
F
Pray, praise and sing "Hurray!"
     C7   F
Her father loved her so.

F
Her mother loved her so,
F
Her mother loved her so.
F
Pray, praise and sing "Hurray!"
     C7   F
Her mother loved her so.

F
The little girl has died,
F
The little girl has died.
F
We are all so very sad.
     C7   F
The little girl has died.

F
Now Jesus loves her so,
F
Now Jesus loves her so.
F
Pray, praise and sing "Hurray!"
     C7   F
Now Jesus loves her so.

F
The little girl's alive!
F
The little girl's alive!
F
Pray, praise and sing "Hurray!"
     C7   F
The little girl's alive!

Lois Watt and
June Meier
St. Libory, NE

LAZARUS LIVES

Sung to: "Frere Jacques"

C
We are sad, we are sad,
C
Yes, we are; yes, we are.
C
Lazarus has died,
C
Lazarus has died.
C
Boo, hoo, hoo; boo, hoo, hoo.

C
We are happy, we are happy,
C
Lazarus lives, Lazarus lives.
C
Jesus Christ has raised him,
C
Jesus Christ has raised him.
C
Smile, smile, smile; smile, smile, smile.

Becky Gogel
Costa Mesa, CA

JESUS FED THE FIVE THOUSAND

Sung to: "For He's a Jolly Good Fellow"

>   C   F   C
> Oh, Jesus fed the five thousand,
>   G7   C
> Oh, Jesus fed the five thousand,
>   C   F
> Oh, Jesus fed the five thousand.
>   G7   C
> He fed them one fine day.

>   C   F C
> He had five loaves and two fishes,
>   G7   C
> He had five loaves and two fishes,
>   C   F
> He had five loaves and two fishes.
> G7   C
> That is all He had.

>   C   F C
> They all had eaten plenty,
>   G7   C
> They all had eaten plenty,
>   C   F
> They all had eaten plenty.
>   G7   C
> The food still overflowed.

>   C   F C
> How did He ever do it?
>   G7   C
> How did He ever do it?
>   C   F
> How did He ever do it?
>   G7   C
> He put His trust in God.

Judy Hall
Wytheville, VA

FIVE LITTLE LOAVES

Sung to: "Ten Little Indians"

> C
> Five little loaves and two little fishes,
> G
> Five little loaves and two little fishes,
> C
> Five little loaves and two little fishes
> G   C
> In the little boy's lunch.

> C
> Five little loaves and two little fishes,
> G
> Five little loaves and two little fishes,
> C
> Five little loaves and two little fishes.
> G   C
> Jesus fed the bunch.

Janet Harris
Annandale, NJ

FEEDING THE FIVE THOUSAND

Sung to: "Three Blind Mice"

> C   G   C   C   G   C
> Two small fish, two small fish,
> C   G   C   C   G   C
> Five loaves of bread, five loaves of bread.
>   C   G   C
> They all were given by one little lad,
>   C   G   C
> He gave to Jesus the food he had.
> C   G   C
> Jesus blessed the food that day.
> C   G   C
> Five thousand people were fed.

Mary Evelyn Barcus
Indianapolis, IN

THOMAS THE DOUBTER

Sung to: "Did You Ever See a Lassie?"

    F
Oh, Jesus came to Thomas,
  C7   F
To Thomas, who doubted.
    F
Oh, Jesus came to Thomas,
    C7   F
And Thomas believed.

    F
We all need to trust Him,
    C7   F
And He will guide us.
    F
Oh, Jesus comes to all
    C7   F
Who want to believe.

> Rachel Kramer
> Beulah, ND

MIRACLES

Sung to: "When the Saints Go Marching In"

        D
There was a boy who shared his lunch,
          A7
On a busy, sunny day.
    D   G
Jesus took it and fed five thousand,
    D A7   D
On a busy, sunny day.

         D
There was a man who never walked,
          A7
On a busy, sunny day.
    D   G
Jesus put His hand upon him,
      D   A7   G
And he ran home all the way.

> Florence Dieckmann
> Roanoke, VA

ZACCHAEUS

Sung to: "Mary Had a Little Lamb"

F
Zacchaeus was a little man,
C7   F
Little man, little man.
F
Zacchaeus was a little man.
C7   F
He was very short.

        F
He wanted to see Christ go by,
C7   F
Christ go by, Christ go by.
        F
He wanted to see Christ go by,
C7   F
So he climbed a tree.

F
Jesus stopped and looked at him,
C7   F
Looked at him, looked at him.
F
Jesus stopped and looked at him
      C7   F
And then said, "Come on down."

F
"I will go to your home,
C7   F
To your home, to your home.
F
I will go to your home,
     C7   F
And I will dine with you."

> Teri Muller
> Westminster, MD

THE HOUSE BUILT ON ROCK

Sung to: "Mary Had a Little Lamb"

F
There was a house built on the sand,
C7   F
On the sand, on the sand.
F
There was a house built on the sand,
C7   F
Built by a certain man.

      F
The waters came and it fell down,
C7   F
It fell down, it fell down.
      F
The waters came and it fell down,
    C7   F
The house he built on sand.

        F
There was a house built on a rock,
C7   F
On a rock, on a rock.
        F
There was a house built on a rock,
C7   F
Built by another man.

      F
The waters came and it held firm,
C7   F
It held firm, it held firm.
      F
The waters came and it held firm,
    C7   F
Because it was built on rock.

      F
So build your faith on Jesus Christ,
C7   F
Jesus Christ, Jesus Christ.
      F
So build your faith on Jesus Christ,
    C7   F
Because He never fails.

Becky Gogel
Costa Mesa, CA

SONGS ABOUT CHRISTMAS

GOING TO BETHLEHEM

Sung to: "Mary Had a Little Lamb"

F
Mary rode a donkey,
   C7   F
A donkey, a donkey.
F
Mary rode a donkey,
C7   F
Going to Bethlehem.

F
Joseph walked beside her,
   C7   F
Beside her, beside her.
F
Joseph walked beside her,
C7   F
Going to Bethlehem.

Janet Harris
Annandale, NJ

LONG AGO

Sung to: "Row, Row, Row Your Boat"

C
Long, long, long ago,
C
An angel came to say,
C
"Mary, Mary, you will have
   G   C
A babe on Christmas Day."

C
Long, long, long ago,
C
The angel's words came true.
C
Baby Jesus came to be
   G   C
A friend for me and you.

Janet Harris
Annandale, NJ

HIS NAME WAS JESUS

Sung to: "London Bridge"

F
Mary had a baby boy,
C7   F
Baby boy, baby boy.
F
Mary had a baby boy.
   C7   F
His name was Jesus.

F
Shepherds came to see the child,
C7   F
See the child, see the child.
F
Shepherds came to see the child.
   C7   F
His name was Jesus.

Vicki Shannon
Napton, MO

MARY HAD A BABY BOY

Sung to: "Mary Had a Little Lamb"

F
Mary had a baby boy,
C7   F
Baby boy, baby boy.
F
Mary had a baby boy,
     C7   F
And Jesus was His name.

     F
She wrapped Him up in swaddling clothes,
C7   F
Swaddling clothes, swaddling clothes.
     F
She wrapped Him up in swaddling clothes
     C7   F
And laid Him in the hay.

     F
He came to show us God's great love,
C7   F
God's great love, God's great love.
     F
He came to show us God's great love
     C7   F
On that first Christmas Day.

Linda Warren
Newbury Park, CA

ON CHRISTMAS DAY

Sung to: "The Mulberry Bush"

C
Jesus was born in Bethlehem,
  G7
In Bethlehem, in Bethlehem.
C
Jesus was born in Bethlehem,
  G7   C
On Christmas Day in the morning.

Sr. Christine Yurick, VSC
Pittsburgh, PA

BABY JESUS

Sung to: "Frere Jacques"

C
Baby Jesus, Baby Jesus
C
Was born to, was born to
C
Mary and Joseph,
C
Mary and Joseph,
C
On this day, Christmas Day.

C
Mary held Him, Mary held Him
C
In her arms, in her arms.
C
She loved her tiny baby,
C
She fed her tiny baby.
C
Christ was born, Christ was born.

C
As He grew, as He grew,
C
God did speak, God did teach,
C
Showing us the way,
C
Guiding us each day.
C
His light shines through on me and you.

Saundra Winnett
Lewisville, TX

MARY AND JOSEPH

Sung to: "Ten Little Indians"

C
Mary and Joseph went to Bethlehem,

G
Mary and Joseph went to Bethlehem,

C
Mary and Joseph went to Bethlehem,

G   C
Riding on a donkey.

C
All the inns were full of travelers,

G
All the inns were full of travelers,

C
All the inns were full of travelers.

     G   C
There was no room for Mary.

C
So they rested in a stable,

G
So they rested in a stable,

C
So they rested in a stable.

G   C
They could go no farther.

C
Baby Jesus was born to Mary,

G
Baby Jesus was born to Mary,

C
Baby Jesus was born to Mary.

     G   C
She laid Him in a manger.

C
Shepherds tending flocks on the hillside,

G
Shepherds tending flocks on the hillside,

C
Shepherds tending flocks on the hillside

G   C
Heard the news from the angels.

C
A star shone brightly o'er the stable,

G
A star shone brightly o'er the stable,

C
A star shone brightly o'er the stable,

G   C
Where the babe was sleeping.

C
Wise Men traveled from the Orient,

G
Wise Men traveled from the Orient,

C
Wise Men traveled from the Orient,

G   C
Bringing gifts to Jesus.

C
Now we celebrate Jesus' birthday,

G
Now we celebrate Jesus' birthday,

C
Now we celebrate Jesus' birthday

G   C
On each Christmas Day.

Marueen Gutyan
Williams Lake, B.C.

JESUS WAS BORN IN BETHLEHEM

Sung to: "Mary Had a Little Lamb"

F
Jesus was born in Bethlehem,
C7   F
Bethlehem, Bethlehem.
F
Jesus was born in Bethlehem,
C7   F
Many years ago.

F
Shepherds heard the angels say,
C7   F
Angels say, angels say,
F
Shepherds heard the angels say
    C7   F
Our King is born this day.

F
Wise Men followed a shining star,
C7   F
Shining star, shining star.
F
Wise Men followed a shining star
    C7   F
And traveled very far.

    F
What presents can we offer Him,
C7   F
Offer Him, offer Him?
    F
What presents can we offer Him?
    C7   F
We'll give the gift of love.

F
Join us all now as we sing,
C7   F
As we sing, as we sing.
F
Join us all now as we sing
    C7   F
In praise of our new King.

Deborah A. Roessel
Flemington, NJ

CHRIST WAS BORN

Sung to: "Mary Had a Little Lamb"

F
Christ was born on Christmas Day,
C7   F
Christmas Day, Christmas Day.
F
Christ was born on Christmas Day,
    C7   F
God's gift of love to us.

Barbara Dunn
Hollidaysburg, PA

CHRISTMAS JOY

Sung to: "I'm a Little Teapot"

G   C   G
Christmas here and Christmas there,
C   G   D7   G
Christmas joy is everywhere.
G   C   G
Baby Jesus came from up above
    C   G   D7   G
To give all people God's great love.

Karen Vollmer
Wauseon, OH

27

MARY HAD A LITTLE BABY

Sung to: "Mary Had a Little Lamb"

F
Mary had a little baby,
C7   F
Little baby, little baby.
F
Mary had a little baby.
C7   F
Jesus was His name.

F
He was born in Bethlehem,
C7   F
Bethlehem, Bethlehem.
F
He was born in Bethlehem
C7   F
On Christmas Day.

F
All the shepherds came to see,
C7   F
Came to see, came to see,
F
All the shepherds came to see
C7   F
The newborn King.

   F
The Wise Men came with their gifts,
C7   F
With their gifts, with their gifts.
   F
The Wise Men came with their gifts,
C7 F
So to honor Him.

   F
And so we, too, can celebrate,
C7 F
Celebrate, celebrate.
   F
And so we, too, can celebrate.
C7   F
Happy Birthday!

Karen Steinfeld,
Pine Island, NY

CHRISTMAS TIME

Sung to: "Twinkle, Twinkle, Little Star"

C   F C
Jesus' birthday time is here,
F C G C
Time for love and time for cheer.
C G C G
Christmas means to celebrate,
C G C   G7
After such a long, long wait.
C   F C
Share God's love with all you know,
F C G7 C
Let your Christmas spirit show!

Karen Leslie
Erie, PA

CHRISTMAS BELLS

Sung to: "Mary Had a Little Lamb"

F
Christmas bells are ringing out,
C   F
Ringing out, ringing out.
F
Christmas bells are ringing out,
C   F
Jesus Christ is born.

F
Angels told the shepherds,
     C   F
The shepherds, the shepherds,
F
Angels told the shepherds,
C   F
Jesus Christ is born.

F
Shepherds came to worship Him,
C   F
Worship Him, worship Him.
F
Shepherds came to worship Him,
C   F
Jesus Christ is born.

Carol Lane
Carol Stream, IL

THE GREATEST GIFT

Sung to: "This Old Man"

C
We get gifts, oh, so fine,
F   G
From our friends at Christmas time.
       C
But God gave us the greatest gift, you see.
G   C G C
He gave Jesus for you and me.

Neva Troyer
Mason City, IA

BELLS ARE RINGING

Sung to: "Frere Jacques"

C
Bells are ringing, children singing,
C
Christmas is here, Christmas is here.
C
Happy Birthday, Jesus,
C
Happy Birthday, Jesus.
C
We love you, we love you.

Marlene V. Filsinger
Snyder, NY

JESUS TAUGHT SHARING

Sung to: "It's Raining, It's Pouring"

C
Jesus taught sharing,
C
Loving and caring.
G7
That's why we're all sharing
             C
Our love at Christmas time.

Diantha Gross
Franklin, NH

THE GREATEST STORY

Sung to: "Eensy, Weensy Spider"

    F
The little Baby Jesus
   C   F
Was born upon the hay.
   F
Along came the angel sending
C   F
Shepherds on their way.
F
Out came the bright star
   C   F
For Wise Men and their gold.
     F
And that is the greatest
C   F
Story ever told.

Gayle Wiemeyer
York, PA

SONG OF THE SHEPHERDS

Sung to: "Braham's Lullaby"

       C
Lay your head on the hay,
            G7
Go to sleep, Baby Jesus.
   G7
Angels watch you in sleep,
          C
As we kneel by your side.
     F   C
Praise to God for His gift,
   G7   C
May your slumber be blessed.
    F   C
Thanks to God for His gift
   G7   C
To His children on earth.

Jackie Owen
Fort Worth, TX

THE SHEPHERD'S LAMB

Sung to: "Mary Had a Little Lamb"

     F
The shepherd had a little lamb,
C7   F
Little lamb, little lamb.
     F
The shepherd had a little lamb.
   C7   F
He watched it every day.

F
Everywhere the shepherd went,
C7   F
Shepherd went, shepherd went,
F
Everywhere the shepherd went,
   C7   F
The lamb would run and play.

      F
He took the lamb to Bethlehem,
C7   F
Bethlehem, Bethlehem.
     F
He took the lamb to Bethlehem,
   C7   F
Where Baby Jesus lay.

Karen Vollmer
Wauseon, OH

CHRISTMAS STAR

Sung to: "Twinkle, Twinkle, Little Star"

C   F   C
Twinkle, twinkle, little star,
F   C   G   C
Shining brightly from afar.
C   F   C   G
Guiding Wise Men on their way,
C   F   C   G7
Showing them where Jesus lay.
C   F   C
Twinkle, twinkle, little star,
F   C   G7   C
Shining brightly from afar.

Cindy Dingwall
Palatine, IL

TWINKLE, TWINKLE, SPECIAL STAR

Sung to: "Twinkle, Twinkle, Little Star"

C   F   C
Twinkle, twinkle, special star,
F   C   G7   C
Wise Men saw you from afar.
C   F   C   G7
Riding camels night and day
C   F   C   G7
To the manger where He lay.
C   F   C
Bearing gifts, they came to see
G7   C   G7   C
Jesus born for you and me.

Jackie Owen
Fort Worth, TX

LEAD US

Sung to: "Twinkle, Twinkle, Little Star"

C   F   C
Twinkle, twinkle, little star,
F   C   G   C
Lead us to our Savior's door.
C   G   C   G
Shine so bright, shine so clear,
C   G   C   G7
Show the world that He is here.
C   F   C
Twinkle, twinkle, little star,
F   C   G7   C
Lead us to our Savior's door.

Barbara Dunn
Hollidaysburg, PA

LULLABY FOR JESUS

Sung to: "Twinkle, Twinkle, Little Star"

C   F   C
Hush, my baby, do not cry,
F   C   G7   C
In the manger where you lie.
C   F   C   G7
Up above a new star shines,
C   F   C   G7
Bringing joy to all mankind.
C   F   C
Listen, Baby, angels sing,
F   C   G7   C
You're our special newborn King.

Vicki Claybrook
Kennewick, WA

CAMELS AND WISE MEN

Sung to: "Frere Jacques"

C
We are camels, we are camels,

C
Gold and brown, gold and brown,

C
Following the leader,

C
Going to see Jesus.

C
Come along, come along.

C
We are Wise Men, we are Wise Men,

C
From afar, from afar,

C
Following the bright star,

C
Bearing gifts for Jesus.

C
Come along, come along.

Jackie Owen
Fort Worth, TX

JESUS WAS BORN ON CHRISTMAS DAY

Sung to: "Hush, Little Baby"

F   C7
Jesus was born on Christmas Day,

              F
His mother laid Him on the hay.

F   C7
Angels did their glory sing,

C7   F
Shepherds all their sheep did bring.

F   C7
Three Wise Men did see the star,

C7   F
Followed it many days from afar

F   C7
To the place where Jesus lay,

C7   F
On His little bed of hay.

Jill Behnke
Hastings, MN

SING A SONG FOR JESUS

Sung to: "Sing a Song of Sixpence"

C
Sing a song for Jesus,

    G7
The King is born today.

G7
Wise Men from afar

C
Bring gifts along the way.

C
"Glory to our God"

    G7
And "Peace on earth" we sing.

G7
Jesus Christ was sent to us

            C
To be our Savior King.

Judy Hall
Wytheville, VA

HERE WE GO TO BETHLEHEM

Sung to: "The Mulberry Bush"

C
Here we go to Bethlehem,
G7
Bethlehem, Bethlehem.
C
Here we go to Bethlehem
  G7   C
To see the newborn King.

  C
The Wise Men came from far away,
G7
Far away, far away.
  C
The Wise Men came from far away.
G7   C
Gifts the three did bring.

C
All bow down and worship Him,
G7
Worship Him, worship Him.
C
All bow down and worship Him.
G7   C
Praises we will sing.

     Judy Hall
     Wytheville, VA

NINE LITTLE ANGELS

Sung to: "Ten Little Indians"

C
One little, two little, three little angels,
G
Four little, five little, six little angels,
C
Seven little, eight little, nine little angels
G   C
Watching Baby Jesus!

     Jean Anderson
     St. Paul, MN

A WONDROUS CHILD

Sung to: "Davy Crockett"

C   F
Born in Bethlehem, a manger small,
C   G
With the animals, short and tall.
C   F
The angel said, "Come one and all,
  G7   C
The King is born today in a little stall."

Chorus:
C   F C
Jesus — Baby Jesus,
G   C
Born on Christmas Day.

C   F
The shepherds came and the Wise Men, too,
C   G
Bringing gifts to the babe so new,
C   F
Gold and myrrh, to name a few.
  G7   C
A wondrous child was born which they all knew.

Chorus

     Judy Hall
     Wytheville, VA

CHRIST WAS BORN TODAY

Sung to: "Jingle Bells"

C
Christ was born, Christ was born,
C
Christ was born today.
     F   C
God sent His Son to be our friend
     D7   G
And help us every day.
C
Christ was born, Christ was born,
C
Christ was born today.
     F   C
God sent His Son to be our friend
     G7   C
And help in every way.

Lori Gross
Souderton, PA

THE LORD IS BORN TODAY

Sung to: "The Farmer in the Dell"

     F
The Lord is born today,
     F
The Lord is born today.
     F
He left His throne to make a home
          C   F
In a stable, on the hay.

Barbara Dunn
Hollidaysburg, PA

A SAVIOR BORN

Sung to: "Bingo"

  F   Bb   F
A Savior born on Christmas Day,
  F   C7   F
And Jesus is His name-o.
F   Bb   C7   F   F   Bb
J-E-S-U-S, J-E-S-U-S, J-E-S-U-S,
    C7   F
And Jesus is His name-o.

F   Bb   F
Wise men still seek Him today,
    F   G7   F
And Jesus is His name-o.
F   Bb   C7   F   F   Bb
J-E-S-U-S, J-E-S-U-S, J-E-S-U-S,
    C7   F
And Jesus is His name-o.

Marie Wheeler
Tacoma, WA

HURRAY! HURRAY! HURRAY!

Sung to: "The Mulberry Bush"

C
Jesus was born on Christmas Day,
G7
Christmas Day, Christmas Day.
C
Jesus was born on Christmas Day.
G7   C
Hurray! Hurray! Hurray!

C
Jesus loves all of us every day,
G7
Every day, every day.
C
Jesus loves all of us every day.
G7   C
Hurray! Hurray! Hurray!

Betty Silkunas
Philadelphia, PA

SONGS ABOUT EASTER

PALM SUNDAY

Sung to: "Mary Had a Little Lamb"

F
Jesus is the Son of God,
C7   F
Son of God, Son of God.
F
Jesus is the Son of God,
C7   F
And we love Him so.

F
He rode into Jerusalem,
C7   F
Jerusalem, Jerusalem.
F
He rode into Jerusalem.
C7   F
The people loved Him so.

F
That was our first Palm Sunday,
C7   F
Palm Sunday, Palm Sunday.
F
That was our first Palm Sunday,
C7   F
Many years ago.

Laura M. Koenig
New Milford, CT

RIDE INTO JERUSALEM

Sung to: "Row, Row, Row Your Boat"

C
Walk, walk, walk along,
C
Going into town.
C
Jesus told the men to get
G   C
A donkey to ride on.

C
Ride, ride, ride upon
C
The donkey that they found.
C
Other people in the crowd
G   C
Threw garments on the ground.

C
Wave, wave, wave the palms,
C
Lift them in the air.
C
Sing your praises as they pass,
G   C
Your King is riding there.

Judy Meyer and
Sharon Vonada
Boca Raton, FL

GETHSEMANE

Sung to: "Row, Row, Row Your Boat"

C
Jesus went alone to pray
C
In Gethsemane.
C
All He wanted was God's love
       G   C
And to share His life with me.

Marlene V. Filsinger
Snyder, NY

JESUS LIVES

Sung to: "Frere Jacques"

C
Here's the cross, here's the cross.
    (Make cross with fingers.)
C
Jesus died, Jesus died.
C
Here's the tomb,
    (Put fingertips together.)
C
Empty tomb.
    (Hold hands out, palms up.)
C
Jesus lives! Jesus lives!
    (Clap out each word.)

Shirley Scott
Orrville, OH

THERE WAS A MAN FROM GALILEE

Sung to: "Bingo"

           F   B♭   F
There was a man from Galilee,
      F   C7   F
And Jesus was His name-o.
F   B♭   C7   F   F   B♭
J-E-S-U-S, J-E-S-U-S, J-E-S-U-S,
       C7   F
And Jesus was His name-o.

       F   B♭   F
He died on the cross to set us free,
      F   C7   F
And Jesus was His name-o.
F   B♭   C7   F   F   B♭
J-E-S-U-S, J-E-S-U-S, J-E-S-U-S,
       C7   F
And Jesus was His name-o.

       F   B♭   F
He rose from the grave in victory,
      F   C7   F
And Jesus was His name-o.
F   B♭   C7   F   F   B♭
J-E-S-U-S, J-E-S-U-S, J-E-S-U-S,
       C7   F
And Jesus was His name-o.

Karen Brown
Bentonville, AR

EASTER SUNDAY

Sung to: "Frere Jacques"

F
Easter Sunday, Easter Sunday,

F
Jesus lives, Jesus lives!

F
See the empty tomb,

F
See the empty tomb.

F
Jesus lives, Jesus lives!

Rachel Kramer
Beulah, ND

JESUS LIVES TODAY

Sung to: "Frere Jacques"

F
Out of the tomb, out of the tomb

F
Jesus came, Jesus came.

F
Jesus lives today,

F
Jesus lives today!

F
Yes, He does! Yes, He does!

Joyce Raymond
Des Moines, IA

EASTER JOY

Sung to: "Row, Row, Row Your Boat"

C
Joy, joy everywhere,

C
Jesus is alive!

C
Rejoice, rejoice, rejoice, rejoice,

G   C
Jesus is alive!

Mary K. Miller
Greenville, PA

HAPPY EASTER

Sung to: "Frere Jacques"

C
He is risen, He is risen,

C
Christ our Lord, Christ our Lord.

C
Happy, Happy Easter,

C
Happy, Happy Easter!

C
Happy Spring, Happy Spring!

Linda I. Grubbs
La Marque, TX

WHERE IS JESUS?

Sung to: "Frere Jacques"

C
Where is Jesus, where is Jesus?

C
He's not here, He's not here.

C
He is risen,

C
He is risen.

C
Jesus lives, Jesus lives!

Jean Scheiwe
Bay City, MI

EASTER BELLS

Sung to: "Mary Had a Little Lamb"

F
Easter bells are ringing out,
C7   F
Ringing out, ringing out.
F
Easter bells are ringing out.
C7   F
Christ is risen today!

Carol Lane
Carol Stream, IL

WHAT IS EASTER?

Sung to: "Frere Jacques"

C
What is Easter, what is Easter?
C
Jesus rose, Jesus rose.
C
He became our Savior,
C
He became our Savior,
C
Easter Day, Easter Day.

Sue Wilke
Seattle, WA

IT IS EASTER

Sung to: "Jack and Jill"

C   G7
It is Easter,
C   G7
We are joyful,
C   F C
Jesus Christ is risen!
G7
Yes, He lives!
        C
His love He gives,
     Dm   G7   C
And we are oh, so thankful!

Vicki Shannon
Napton, MO

EASTER

Sung to: "Mary Had a Little Lamb"

F
Easter is our resurrection,
C7   F
Resurrection, resurrection!
F
Easter is our resurrection,
      C7   F
New life and hope and love!

Sue Schliecker
Waukesha, WI

CHRISTIANS ARE REJOICING

Sung to: "Jack and Jill"

Bb F7 Bb F7
Alleluia! Alleluia!
Bb   Eb Bb
Christians are rejoicing!
F7   Bb
Alleluia! Alleluia!
Cm F7   Bb
Jesus Christ is risen!

> Sr. Christine Yurick, VSC
> Pittsburgh, PA

HE IS RISEN

Sung to: "This Old Man"

C
He is risen, He is risen,
F   G
Lift your hands up to the sky!
       C
And we'll spread the news of our living Lord.
G   C G C
Jesus Christ is risen today!

> Neva Troyer
> Mason City, IA

ALLELUIA

Sung to: "Ten Little Indians"

C
Alleluia, Christ is risen,
G
Alleluia, Christ is risen,
C
Alleluia, Christ is risen!
G   C
Christ is risen today!

> Sue Schliecker
> Waukesha, WI

CLAP YOUR HANDS

Sung to: "London Bridge"

F
Clap your hands and sing for joy,
C7   F
Sing for joy, sing for joy!
F
Clap your hands and sing for joy!
C7   F
Christ is risen!

F
Now we have good news to tell,
C7   F
News to tell, news to tell!
F
Now we have good news to tell!
C7   F
Christ is risen!

> Karen Vollmer
> Wauseon, OH

CHRIST IS RISEN

Sung to: "Frere Jacques"

F
Christ is risen, Christ is risen,
F
Lives again, lives again.
F
Sing "Alleluia!"
F
Sing "Alleluia!"
F
A-men. A-men.

> Karen Vollmer
> Wauseon, OH

SONGS ABOUT LOVE

DID YOU EVER MEET MY JESUS?

Sung to: "Did You Ever See a Lassie?"

      F
Did you ever meet my Jesus,
  C7   F
My Jesus, my Jesus?
      F
Did you ever meet my Jesus?
  C7   F
He really loves you.
   C7   F
He'll lead you and guide you
   C7   F
And stay right beside you.
      F
Did you ever meet my Jesus?
  C7   F
He really loves you.

> Lori Gross
> Souderton, PA

YES, IT'S TRUE

Sung to: "Frere Jacques"

F
Jesus loves you, Jesus loves you,
F
Yes, it's true; yes, it's true.
F
He will lead and guide you,
F
He will lead and guide you.
F
Follow Him, follow Him.

> Lori Gross
> Souderton, PA

JESUS SURE LOVES YOU!

Sung to: "Ten Little Indians"

C
Nod your head if you love Jesus,
G7
Nod your head if you love Jesus,
C
Nod your head if you love Jesus.
G7   C
Jesus sure loves you!

C
Clap your hands if you love Jesus,
G7
Clap your hands if you love Jesus,
C
Clap your hands if you love Jesus.
G7   C
Jesus sure loves you!

C
Stamp your feet if you love Jesus,
G7
Stamp your feet if you love Jesus,
C
Stamp your feet if you love Jesus.
G7   C
Jesus sure loves you!

> Betty Silkunas
> Philadelphia, PA

CHILDREN, LISTEN

Sung to: "Jimmy Crack Corn"

F   C7
Children, listen to what I say,
        F
Jesus loves you every day.
             Bb
Thank Him when you say your prayers,
  C7   F
Because you know He really cares.

> Eleanor Roodenburg
> Geneseo, NY

JESUS LOVES YOU

Sung to: "The Farmer in the Dell"

F
Jesus loves you,
F
Jesus loves you.
F
All day long, the whole night through,
F   C7   F
Jesus loves you.

Karen Miller
South Euclid, OH

JESUS LOVES

Sung to: "Three Blind Mice"

C G C   C G C
Jesus loves, Jesus loves.
C G   C   C G   C
He loves you, He loves me.
    C   G   C
He loves us when we're being good,
    C   G   C
Or when we're not but know we should.
    G   C
He forgives like He said He would.
    C G C
Yes, Jesus loves.

Karen Ernst
Coupeville, WA

JESUS LOVES US

Sung to: "London Bridge"

F
Jesus loves us very much,
C7   F
Very much, very much.
F
Jesus loves us very much.
C7   F
Yes, He does.

Joyce Raymond
Des Moines, IA

JESUS IS KIND TO YOU AND ME

Sung to: "The Mulberry Bush"

C
Jesus is kind to you and me,
G7
You and me, you and me.
C
Jesus is kind to you and me,
    G7   C
So we will be kind, too.

C
Jesus is gentle with you and me,
G7
You and me, you and me.
C
Jesus is gentle with you and me,
    G7   C
So we will be gentle, too.

C
Jesus is patient with you and me,
G7
You and me, you and me.
C
Jesus is patient with you and me,
    G7   C
So we will be patient, too.

C
Jesus always loves you and me,
G7
You and me, you and me.
C
Jesus always loves you and me,
    G7   C
So we will be loving, too.

Kathy Sizer
Tustin, CA

JESUS WAS A LITTLE CHILD

Sung to: "I'm a Little Teapot"

C   F   C
Jesus was a lit-tle child, just like me.
  G   C   G   C
He grew and grew, so soon to be
      C   F   C
The Savior of the world and to love us, too,
F   C   G7   C
Love us all — both me and you!

Louanne Hutcheson
Carrollton, GA

JESUS LOVES YOU AND ME

Sung to: "Happy Birthday"

      F   C
Jesus loves you and me,

(Look upward on "Jesus loves," point outward
on "you" and to self on "me.")
      C   F
Jesus loves you and me.
      F   Bb
In the Bible I read this.

(Cup hands to form a book.)
      F   C   F
Jesus loves you and me.

Repeat substituting children's names for "you" and "me."

Mary K. Miller
Greenville, PA

I AM SO GLAD

Sung to: "Mary Had a Little Lamb"

F
Jesus loves you and me,
C7   F
You and me, you and me.
F
Jesus loves you and me,
    C7   F
And I am so glad.

F
Clap your hands and jump for joy,
C7   F
Jump for joy, jump for joy.
F
Clap your hands and jump for joy.
C7   F
Jesus loves us all.

Teri Muller
Westminster, MD

JESUS LOVES US VERY MUCH

Sung to: "Mary Had a Little Lamb"

F
Jesus loves us very much,
C7   F
Very much, very much.
F
Jesus loves us very much.
    C7   F
He is our special friend.

F
We should try to be like Him,
C7   F
Be like Him, be like Him.
F
We should try to be like Him
    C7   C
By being kind to all.

Jill Behnke
Hastings, MN

JESUS CHRIST

Sung to: "Jingle Bells"

C
Jesus Christ, Jesus Christ,
C
He's the Son of God.
F   C
He's my Lord and Savior, too,
D7   G
He's my special friend.
C
Jesus Christ, Jesus Christ,
C
Loves us all the same.
F   C
He loves you; He loves me, too.
  G7   C
His love will never end.

Jeanette Koelling
Ord, NE

LITTLE CHILDREN

Sung to: "Twinkle, Twinkle, Little Star"

C   F C
Jesus loves us, it is clear,
F   C   G7   C
Little children far and near.
C   F   C   G7
Red, yellow, black and white,
C   F   C   G7
All are precious in His sight.
C   F   C
Jesus loves us all, you see,
F   C   G7   C
He loves you and He loves me!

Judy Hall
Wytheville, VA

JESUS LOVES ME

Sung to: "Frere Jacques"

C
Jesus loves me, Jesus loves me
C
When I work, when I play.
C
He is always with me,
C
He is always with me,
C
Every day, every day.

Karen Brown
Bentonville, AR

JESUS LOVES THE BOYS AND GIRLS

Sung to: "London Bridge"

F
Jesus loves the boys and girls,
C7   F
Yes, He does; yes, He does.
F
Jesus loves the boys and girls.
C7   F
Yes, He loves us!

Rachel Kramer
Beulah, ND

CHILDREN OF THE WORLD

Sung to: "Alouette"

Chorus:

C
Jesus loves them,

G7   C
Children, yes, He loves them.

C
Jesus loves them,

G7   C
Children of the world.

  C
It doesn't matter where you live,

 G7   C
It doesn't matter where you live.

G
Where you live, where you live, oh —

Chorus

  C
It doesn't matter how you speak,

 G7   C
It doesn't matter how you speak.

G7
How you speak, how you speak,

G7
Where you live, where you live, oh —

Chorus

  C
It doesn't matter how you dress,

 G7   C
It doesn't matter how you dress.

G7
How you dress, how you dress,

G7
How you speak, how you speak,

G7
Where you live, where you live, oh —

Chorus

Judy Hall
Wytheville, VA

YES, HE DOES

Sung to: "Frere Jacques"

C
Jesus loves me, Jesus loves me,

C
Yes, He does; yes, He does.

C
He will stay beside me,

C
He will always guide me.

C
Thank you, Lord; thank you, Lord.

Debra Lindahl
Libertyville, IL

WHEN I'M SAD

Sung to: "Frere Jacques"

C
When I'm sad or when I'm frightened,

C
Jesus cares, Jesus cares.

C
I don't have to cry,

C
I don't have to cry.

C
He is there, He is there.

Jewel A. Stevens, M.D.
Springboro, OH

JESUS HAS A LITTLE LAMB

Sung to: "Mary Had a Little Lamb"

F
Jesus has a little lamb,
C7   F
Little lamb, little lamb.
F
Jesus has a little lamb.
     C7   F
That little lamb is me.

F
Everywhere I'll follow Him,
C7   F
Follow Him, follow Him.
F
Everywhere I'll follow Him,
     C7   F
Wherever He may lead.

F
I know that He'll take care of me,
C7   F
Care of me, care of me.
F
I know that He'll take care of me,
     C7   F
Because He loves me so.

Kathy Crawford
Hodgenville, KY

IT SAYS SO IN THE BIBLE

Sung to: "Skip to My Lou"

F
Jesus loves me; yes, He does,
C7
Jesus loves me; yes, He does,
F
Jesus loves me; yes, He does.
     C7   F
It says so in the Bible.

F
He walks beside me every day,
C7
He walks beside me every day,
F
He walks beside me every day.
     C7   F
It says so in the Bible.

F
He protects me, this I know,
C7
He protects me, this I know,
F
He protects me, this I know.
     C7   F
It says so in the Bible.

Neva Troyer
Mason City, IA

I'M A CHILD OF JESUS

Sung to: "I'm a Little Teapot"

G   C   G
I'm a child of Jesus, and I know
C   G   D7   G
He won't forget me, He loves me so.
                    C   G
When I get all worried, frightened or sad,
     C   D7   G
Jesus helps me and makes me glad.

Vicki L. Gilliam
Marlin, TX

YES, I KNOW

Sung to: "Frere Jacques"

C
Jesus loves me, Jesus loves me,
C
Yes, I know; yes, I know.
C
I read it in the Bible,
C
I read it in the Bible.
C
It tells me so, it tells me so.

Betty Ruth Baker
Waco, TX

HE LOVES ME ALL THE TIME

Sung to: "Mary Had a Little Lamb"

F
Jesus loves me when I'm sad,
C7   F
When I'm mad, when I'm bad.
F
Jesus loves me when I'm glad.
C7   F
He loves me all the time.

Marlene V. Filsinger
Snyder, NY

I'M A CHRISTIAN

Sung to: "Frere Jacques"

C
I'm a Christian, I'm a Christian,
C
I believe! I believe!
C
Jesus Christ is special,
C
Jesus Christ is special.
C
He loves me! He loves me!

Sue Schliecker
Waukesha, WI

JESUS IS MY LORD

Sung to: "Jingle Bells"

C
Jesus is my Lord,
              F
I serve Him every day.
              G7
He knows my every need
                    C
And hears me when I pray.
C
No other friend I know
                    F
Could love me like He does.
                C
I want to tell the whole wide world
F   G7   C
How glad I am because —
C
Jesus lives, Jesus lives
C
In my heart today.
F   C
Every time I think of Him,
D7   G7
I want to shout and say —
C
Jesus lives, Jesus lives,
C
Yes, I know it's true.
F   C
And if you want Him in your life,
G7   C
He'll live in your heart, too.

Vicki Shannon
Napton, MO

48

IN MY HEART

Sung to: "Frere Jacques"

C
Where is Jesus, where is Jesus?
C
In my heart, in my heart.
C
I love Him,
C
He loves me.
C
I'm so glad, I'm so glad.

Jeanette Koelling
Ord, NE

I'M A LITTLE FRIEND OF JESUS'

Sung to: "I'm a Yankee Doodle Dandy"

F   G7
I'm a little friend of Jesus',
C7   F
He's a special friend of mine.
     D7   Gm   D7 Gm
He loves me like no other friend I know,
G7   C7
He's with me all of the time.
F   G7
I'm a little friend of Jesus',
C7   F
I know that He is always near.
                              C7
God loved us so much he sent
     F
His Son so we could know Him.
G7   C7   F
Jesus, my friend, is always here.

Vicki L. Gilliam
Marlin, TX

JESUS LOVES ME LIKE I A

Sung to: "London Bridge"

F
Jesus loves me like I am,
C7   F
Like I am, like I am.
F
He's my friend, I trust in Him.
C7   F
Yes, Jesus loves me.

Jan Ebmeier
Hutchinson, KS

I AM HIS

Sung to: "Frere Jacques"

C
Jesus loves me, Jesus loves me
C
All the time, all the time.
C
I belong to Jesus,
C
I belong to Jesus.
C
I am His, I am His.

C
I love Jesus, I love Jesus
C
All the time, all the time.
C
I tell Him when I pray,
C
I tell Him when I pray.
C
I am His, I am His.

Sandy Gogel
Costa Mesa, CA

... A FRIEND

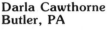

Sung to: "If You're Happy and You Know It"

    F   C7
Oh, I have a friend and Jesus is His name,

                                   F
Oh, I have a friend and Jesus is His name.

    Bb
He is with me night and day,

      F
And He helps me when I pray.

    C7   F
Oh, I have a friend and Jesus is His name.

Darla Cawthorne
Butler, PA

HE'S MY FRIEND FOREVER

Sung to: "Frere Jacques"

C
I love Jesus, I love Jesus,

C
Yes, I do; yes, I do.

C
He's my friend forever,

C
He's my friend forever.

C
It is true, it is true.

Connie Gillilan
Hardy, NE

JESUS IS A FRIEND

Sung to: "The Muffin Man"

G
Jesus is a friend of mine,

  C   D7
A friend of mine, a friend of mine.

G
Jesus is a friend of mine.

  D7   G
He loves me all the time.

G
Jesus loves me when I'm sad,

    (Make sad face and pretend to wipe away tears.)

C   D7
When I'm sad, when I'm sad.

G
Jesus loves me when I'm sad.

  D7   G
He loves me all the time.

Additional verses: "Jesus loves me when I'm happy; mad; scared." Have children make appropriate faces and movements when singing each verse.

Shirley Scott
Orrville, OH

JESUS IS A FRIEND OF MINE

Sung to: "Old MacDonald Had a Farm"

F   Bb   F
Jesus is a friend of mine,

         C7   F
And I love Him so.

F   Bb   F
He just makes me feel so fine,

         C7   F
And I love Him so.

      F
He will walk with me,

        F
And He'll talk with me,

F
Every day, all the way,

F
Everywhere I go, oh —

         Bb   F
Jesus is a friend of mine,

    C7   F
And I love Him so.

Judy Hall
Wytheville, VA

JESUS IS HIS NAME

Sung to: "Bingo"

    F   Bb   F
I have a friend who loves me so,
          C7   F
And Jesus is His na-ame.
F   Bb   C7 F   Bb
J-E-S-U-S, J-E-S-U-S, J-E-S-U-S,
    C7   F
And Jesus is His name!

    F   Bb   F
I have a friend who loves me so,
          C7   F
And Jesus is His na-ame.
F   Bb
J-E-S-U-(clap),
C7 F
J-E-S-U-(clap),
    Bb
J-E-S-U-(clap),
   C7   F
And Jesus is His name!

    F   Bb   F
I have a friend who loves me so,
          C7   F
And Jesus is His na-ame.
F   Bb
J-E-S-(clap, clap),
C7 F
J-E-S-(clap, clap),
    Bb
J-E-S-(clap, clap),
   C7   F
And Jesus is His name!

    F   Bb   F
I have a friend who loves me so,
          C7   F
And Jesus is His na-ame.
F   Bb
J-E-(clap, clap, clap),
C7 F
J-E-(clap, clap, clap),
    Bb
J-E-(clap, clap, clap),
   C7   F
And Jesus is His name!

    F   Bb   F
I have a friend who loves me so,
          C7   F
And Jesus is His na-ame.
F   Bb
J-(clap, clap, clap, clap),
C7   F
J-(clap, clap, clap, clap),
    Bb
J-(clap, clap, clap, clap),
   C7   F
And Jesus is His name!

    F   Bb   F
I have a friend who loves me so,
          C7   F
And Jesus is His na-ame.
F   Bb
(Clap, clap, clap, clap, clap),
C7   F
(Clap, clap, clap, clap, clap),
     Bb
(Clap, clap, clap, clap, clap),
   C7   F
And Jesus is His name!

Cindy Dingwall
Palatine, IL

JESUS IS MY BEST FRIEND

Sung to: "Mary Had a Little Lamb"

F
Jesus is my best friend,
     C7   F
My best friend, my best friend.
F
Jesus is my best friend,
C7   F
And he always cares.

F
Jesus is my best friend,
     C7   F
My best friend, my best friend.
F
Jesus is my best friend,
C7   F
And He's your friend, too.

F
Jesus is my best friend,
     C7   F
My best friend, my best friend.
F
Jesus is my best friend,
C7   F
And He's (child's name)'s friend, too.

Jackie Owen
Fort Worth, TX

MY BEST FRIEND

Sung to: "Did You Ever See a Lassie?"

    F
Oh, Jesus is my best friend,
  C7   F
My best friend, my best friend.
    F
Oh, Jesus is my best friend,
    C7   F
And I love Him so.
  C7   F
He helps me and guides me,
  C7   F
He walks right beside me.
    F
Oh, Jesus is my best friend,
    C7   F
And I love Him so.

Elizabeth McKinnon

JESUS IS MY FRIEND

Sung to: "Row, Row, Row Your Boat"

C
Jesus is my friend,
C
And all through my days,
   C
At school and play and sleep at night,
G   C
By my side He stays.

Marlene V. Filsinger
Snyder, NY

I LOVE JESUS

Sung to: "Skip to My Lou"

F
I love Jesus; yes, I do,
C7
I love Jesus; yes, I do,
F
I love Jesus; yes, I do.
C7   F
Now my life is made anew.

F
Open your heart and let Christ in,
C7
Open your heart and let Christ in,
F
Open your heart and let Christ in.
C7   F
You will find a peace within.

Teri Muller
Westminster, MD

LOVING JESUS

Sung to: "London Bridge"

F
Loving Jesus every day,
C7   F
Every day, every day,
F
He will guide me all the way.
C7   F
My friend Jesus.

F
If to Him you give your heart,
C7   F
Give your heart, give your heart,
        F
He'll help you make a brand new start.
C7   F
Your friend Jesus.

Judy Hall
Wytheville, VA

I LOVE HIM

Sung to: "Skip to My Lou"

F
I love Him, how 'bout you?
C7
I love Him, how 'bout you?
F
I love Him, how 'bout you?
C7   F
Jesus Lord and Savior.

F
I'll sing for Him, how 'bout you?
C7
I'll sing for Him, how 'bout you?
F
I'll sing for Him, how 'bout you?
C7   F
Jesus Lord and Savior.

F
I'll live for Him, how 'bout you?
C7
I'll live for Him, how 'bout you?
F
I'll live for Him, how 'bout you?
C7   F
Jesus Lord and Savior.

Barbara Dunn
Hollidaysburg, PA

WE LOVE JESUS

Sung to: "London Bridge"

C
We love Jesus; yes, we do,
G7   C
Yes, we do; yes, we do.
C
We love Jesus; yes, we do.
G7   C
We love Jesus.

C
We know Jesus loves us, too,
G7   C
Loves us, too; loves us, too.
C
We know Jesus loves us, too.
G7   C
We love Jesus.

C
We talk to Jesus when we pray,
G7   C
When we pray, when we pray.
     C
We talk to Jesus when we pray.
G7   C
We love Jesus.

     C
We sing praises to our Lord,
G7   C
To our Lord, to our Lord.
C
We sing praises to our Lord.
G7   C
We love Jesus.

Barbara Fletcher
El Cajon, CA

HOW I LOVE HIM!

Sung to: "Frere Jacques"

C
How I love Him! How I love Him!
C
Jesus Christ, Jesus Christ.
          C
He came to show us God's love,
          C
He came to show us God's love
C
With His life, with His life.

Gloria V. Thomas
Dallas, TX

JESUS IS THE LAMB OF LOVE

Sung to: "Mary Had a Little Lamb"

F
Jesus is the lamb of love,
C7   F
Lamb of love, lamb of love.
F
Jesus is the lamb of love,
C7   F
Sent to us from God above.

F
In my heart His love I've found,
C7   F
Love I've found, love I've found.
F
In my heart His love I've found.
C7   F
Come help spread it all around.

Nora Loy
Largo, FL

54

LOVING JESUS EVERY DAY

Sung to: "Frere Jacques"

C
Loving Jesus, loving Jesus,
C
Every day, every day.
C
He is always there,
C
And He always cares,
C
Every day, every day.

Judy Hall
Wytheville, VA

DO YOU LOVE HIM?

Sung to: "Frere Jacques"

C
Do you love Him, do you love Him,
C
Christ the Lord, Christ the Lord?
C
He was born to save us,
C
If you will believe it.
C
Do it now, do it now.

Barbara Dunn
Hollidaysburg, PA

NINE LITTLE CHILDREN

Sung to: "Ten Little Indians"

C
One little, two little, three little children,
G
Four little, five little, six little children,
C
Seven little, eight little, nine little children
G   C
Loving Christ the Lord.

Jeanette Koelling
Ord, NE

JESUS IS MY SAVIOR

Sung to: "Frere Jacques"

C
I love Jesus, I love Jesus.
C
Don't you, too; don't you, too?
C
Jesus is my Savior,
C
Jesus is my Savior
C
And yours, too; and yours, too!

Cindy Dingwall
Palatine, IL

A SPECIAL VALENTINE

Sung to: "Mary Had a Little Lamb"

F
I have a special valentine,
C7   F
Valentine, valentine.
F
I have a special valentine,
C7   F
And Jesus is His name.

F
I love Him and He loves me,
C7   F
He loves me, He loves me.
F
I love Him and He loves me.
C7   F
He is my valentine.

Carol Lane
Carol Stream, IL

JESUS, GUARD ME

Sung to: "Twinkle, Twinkle, Little Star"

C   F   C
Jesus, guard me through the night,
F   C G7 C
Wake me with the sunshine bright.
C   F C   G7
Guard the children here and there,
C   F C   G7
Guard the children everywhere.
C   F   C
Jesus, guard me through the night,
F   C G7 C
Wake me with the sunshine bright.

Betty Silkunas
Philadelphia, PA

WE ARE NEVER ALONE

Sung to: "My Bonnie Lies Over the Ocean"

   C F C
Whenever I feel afraid,
 C   D7 G
I think of Jesus.
C   F   C
He is always with me.
  F G C
In Him we can trust.

C   F
Jesus, Jesus,
G   C
Loves and cares for us always.
   C   F
With Jesus, with Jesus,
G   C
We are never alone.

Karen Steinfeld
Pine Island, NY

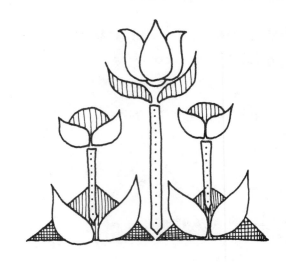

JESUS IS ALWAYS HERE

Sung to: "Frere Jacques"

F
Where is Jesus, where is Jesus?
F
"I'm right here, I'm right here.
F
I am always with you,
F
Whenever you need me.
F
I'm right here, I'm right here."

Rhonda Torres
Ridgecrest, CA

JESUS IS OUR SHEPHERD

Sung to: "I'm a Little Teapot"

G
Jesus is our shepherd,
C   G
We're His sheep.
  C   G
He guides and protects us,
D7   G
Does not sleep.
G   C G
If we wander from the flock at all,
  C   G D7 G
He brings us back so we won't fall.

Judy Hall
Wytheville, VA

SONGS ABOUT FRIENDSHIP AND GOODNESS

FRIENDS AT SCHOOL

Sung to: "Mary Had a Little Lamb"

F
Sharing with my friends at school,
C7   F
Friends at school, friends at school,
F
Sharing with my friends at school,
C7   F
That's the Golden Rule.

F
Playing with my friends at school,
C7   F
Friends at school, friends at school,
F
Playing with my friends at school,
  C7   F
That's what I like to do.

F
Praying with my friends at school,
C7   F
Friends at school, friends at school,
F
Praying with my friends at school,
  C7   F
That's what Christians do.

Lois Olson
Webster City, IA

TEN LITTLE FRIENDS

Sung to: "Ten Little Indians"

C
One little, two little, three little friends,
G
Four little, five little, six little friends,
C
Seven little, eight little, nine little friends,
G   C
Ten little friends at (school/church).

C
I like to share with my friends,
G
I like to share with my friends,
C
I like to share with my friends.
G   C
We have fun at (school/church).

Additional verses: Substitute words such as these for "share": "play, work, sing, laugh."

Karen Vollmer
Wauseon, OH

JESUS TELLS YOU TO

Sung to: "Row, Row, Row Your Boat"

C
Love, love, love your friends,
C
Jesus tells you to.
C
He will help you care for them
G   C
Like He cares for you.

Sue Wilke
Seattle, WA

58

HAPPY GIRLS AND BOYS

Sung to: "Twinkle, Twinkle, Little Star"

C   F C
Happy, happy girls and boys,
F   C G7   C
Help each other, share your toys.
C   F C G7
Making Jesus happy, too,
C F C   G7
For the Bible tells you to.
C   F C
Happy, happy girls and boys,
G7   C G7   C
Help each other, share your toys.

       Rachel Kramer
       Beulah, ND

BE MY FRIEND

Sung to: "Jingle Bells"

C
Come with me, be my friend,
C
Jesus loves us all.
F   C
Oh, what fun it is to have
D7   G
Friends that we can call.
C
We will share, we'll be kind,
C
Jesus shows the way.
F   C
Oh, how happy we will be
  G7   C
When we go out to play!

      Mary K. Miller
      Greenville, PA

WE SHOULD LOVE EACH OTHER

Sung to: "Did You Ever See a Lassie?"

     F
Oh, we should love each other,
     C7   F
Each other, each other.
     F
Oh, we should love each other
     C7   F
Like Jesus loves us.
     C7   F
The tall ones, the short ones,
     C7   F
The fat ones, the skinny ones.
     F
Oh, we should love each other
     C7   F
Like Jesus loves us.

     F
Oh, we should love each other,
     C7   F
Each other, each other.
     F
Oh, we should love each other
     C7   F
Like Jesus loves us.
     C7   F
The old ones, the young ones,
     C7   F
And all of the middle ones.
     F
Oh, we should love each other
     C7   F
Like Jesus loves us.

      Vicki Shannon
      Napton, MO

LOVE

Sung to: "Row, Row, Row Your Boat"

C
Love, love, love the Lord,
    (Cross arms over chest.)
C
That's what Jesus said.
    (Point upward.)
C
Love your neighbor as yourself,
    (Point to another child, then self.)
  G   C
And Jesus will be glad.
    (Point upward with a big smile.)

Mandy Bortz
Chappaqua, NY

I'M A GOOD CHRISTIAN

Sung to: "I'm a Little Teapot"

G
I'm a good Christian,
C   G
Look at me.
C   G   D7   G
I am kind to all I see.
G
When I play with friends,
  C   G
I share my toys.
    C   G   D7   G
I'm good to other girls and boys.

Eleanor Roodenburg
Geneseo, NY

I AM HIS DISCIPLE

Sung to: "Frere Jacques"

C
"Love one another, love one another,"
C
Jesus said, Jesus said.
C
I am His disciple,
C
I am His disciple.
C
I believe! I believe!

Sue Schliecker
Waukesha, WI

BE KIND

Sung to: "The Farmer in the Dell"

F
Jesus said, "Be kind."
F
Jesus said, "Be kind."
      F
So we'll be kind to all our friends.
    C7   F
Jesus said, "Be kind."

F
We like our friends at school,
F
We like our friends at school.
      F
We'll share our toys and playthings, too.
    C7   F
We like our friends at school.

Pauline Laughter
Tulsa, OK

SHOW LOVE TO EVERYONE

Sung to: "Mary Had a Little Lamb"

F
Christians should show God's love,

C7   F
Show God's love, show God's love.

F
Christians should show God's love,

      C7   F
Show love to everyone.

                 Joyce Raymond
                 Des Moines, IA

JESUS SAID

Sung to: "London Bridge"

F
Jesus said that we should be

C7   F
Kind to friends and enemies.

F
Jesus said that we should be

C7   F
Kind to everyone.

F
Jesus said that we should not

    C7   F
Be mean to friends or enemies.

F
Jesus said that we should not

    C7   F
Be mean to anyone.

F
So we'll do what Jesus said,

C7   F
Jesus said, Jesus said.

F
So we'll do what Jesus said.

C7   F
We'll be kind to all.

                 Kathy Sizer
                 Tustin, CA

LET'S BE KIND

Sung to: "London Bridge"

C
Let's be kind to one another,

G7   C
Mother, Father, Sister, Brother.

C
Let's be kind to one another.

G7   C
Jesus said, "Be kind."

                 Betty Silkunas
                 Philadelphia, PA

GUIDING US ALONG THE WAY

Sung to: "Twinkle, Twinkle, Little Star"

C   F   C
Jesus Christ was born one night,

    F   C   G7   C
He came to teach us wrong from right.

C   F   C   G7
Teaching us to love each other,

C   F   C   G7
Mother, Father, Sister, Brother.

       C   F   C
He stays with us every day,

F   C G7   C
Guiding us along the way.

                 Cindy Dingwall
                 Palatine, IL

LIVING LIKE JESUS

Sung to: "Jingle Bells"

C
Jesus is with us,

        F
Teaching us always,

        G7
Helping us to learn

          C
How to live His way.

C
Sharing with our friends,

        F
Taking time to pray,

          C
Listening to our parents who

F   G7   C
Help us grow the right way, oh —

C
Jesus Christ, Jesus Christ,

C
Sent from God above.

     F   C
He came to show us the way

    D7   G7
And to share His love.

C
Jesus Christ, Jesus Christ,

C
Like you we want to live,

F   C
Being kind and helpful,

G7   C
Learning how to give.

Karen Steinfeld
Pine Island, NY

LET'S BE GOOD

Sung to: "Three Blind Mice"

C G C   C G C
We-e should, we-e should

C G C   C G C
All be good, all be good.

        C   G   C
Whenever we're at home or school,

C   G   C
Let's all follow the Golden Rule.

C   G   C
Let's be good like we know we should.

C G C
Let's be good.

Jean Warren

JESUS WAS A GENTLE MAN

Sung to: "The Muffin Man"

G
Jesus was a gentle man,

    C   D7
A gentle man, a gentle man.

G
Jesus was a gentle man,

    D7   G
And I can be like Him.

G
Jesus was a kind man,

    C   D7
A kind man, a kind man.

G
Jesus was a kind man,

    D7   G
And I can be like Him.

Let the children suggest other first lines: "Jesus was a loving man; a patient man; a humble man," etc.

Marion Bergstrom
Kent, WA

HE WAS A CHILD LIKE ME

Sung to: "Pop Goes the Weasel"

D   A7   D
Jesus was a little boy,

    D   A7   D
He was a child like me.

    D   A7
And when His (mom/dad) said,

D
"Help me now,"

A7   D
He did it quickly.

D   A7   D
Jesus was a little boy,

    D   A7   D
He was a child like me.

    D   A7
And when His (mom/dad) said,

D
"Eat your food,"

A7   D
He did it quickly.

D   A7   D
Jesus was a little boy,

    D   A7   D
He was a child like me.

    D   A7
And when His (mom/dad) said,

D
"Do what I say,"

A7   D
He did it quickly.

Jewel A. Stevens, M.D.
Springboro, OH

FRIENDS AND BROTHERS

Sung to: "Michael, Row the Boat Ashore"

C   F   C
Jesus said that we should be friends and brothers,

Em   Dm   G7   C
Jesus said that we should be friends and brothers.

Chorus:

C   F   C
Jesus tells me how to act, I will please Him.

Em   Dm   G7   C
Jesus tells me how to act, I will please Him.

C   F   C
Jesus said that we should not fight one another,

Em   Dm   G7   C
Jesus said that we should not fight one another.

Chorus

C   F   C
Jesus said that we should not hurt one another,

Em   Dm   G7   C
Jesus said that we should not hurt one another.

Chorus

C   F C
Jesus said that we should all tell the truth,

Em   Dm   G7 C
Jesus said that we should all tell the truth.

Chorus

Kathy Sizer
Tustin, CA

WHEN WE PRAY

Sung to: "Mary Had a Little Lamb"

F
Jesus helps us to obey,
C7   F
To obey, to obey.
F
Jesus helps us to obey,
C7   F
When we pray to Him.

F
Jesus takes our sins away,
C7   F
Sins away, sins away.
F
Jesus takes our sins away,
C7   F
When we pray to Him.

F
Jesus gives us peace and joy,
C7   F
Peace and joy, peace and joy.
F
Jesus gives us peace and joy,
C7   F
When we pray to Him.

Becky Gogel
Costa Mesa, CA

MIND YOUR PARENTS

Sung to: "London Bridge"

F
Mind your (mother/father) every day,
C7   F
Every day, every day.
F
Mind your (mother/father) every day.
C7   F
This will make (her/him) happy.

F
Jesus wants us to obey,
C7   F
To obey, to obey.
F
Jesus wants us to obey.
C7   F
This will make Him happy.

Becky Gogel
Costa Mesa, CA

OBEYING JESUS

Sung to: "London Bridge"

F
Jesus has disciples,

C7   F
Disciples, disciples.

F
Jesus has disciples,

C7   F
And you can be one.

F
Follow Jesus every day,

C7   F
Every day, every day.

F
Follow Jesus every day,

C7   F
In every way.

F
Jesus wants us to be kind,

C7   F
To be kind, to be kind.

F
Jesus wants us to be kind,

C7   F
Every day.

F
Jesus wants us to be honest,

C7   F
To be honest, to be honest.

F
Jesus wants us to be honest,

C7   F
Every day.

F
Obey Jesus every day,

C7   F
Every day, every day.

F
Obey Jesus every day,

C7   F
In every way.

Before singing the last verse, add other verses that tell how
Jesus wants us to be.

Cathy Jacobson
Winthrop, WA

BLESSING

Sung to: "Frere Jacques"

C
My dear Jesus, my dear Jesus,

C
Bless my day, bless my day.

C
Help me to be like you,

C
Help me to be Christ-like,

C
In all ways, in all ways.

Susan M. Paprocki
Elmhurst, IL

JESUS WANTS A HELPER

Sung to: "Pop Goes The Weasel"

D   A7   D
Jesus wants a helper today

D   A7   D
And a helper tomorrow.

D   A7   D
Who will be a helper today?

A7   D
Me! Jesus' helper!

Rachel Kramer
Beulah, ND

JESUS WAS A HELPER

Sung to: "Ring Around the Rosie"

C
Jesus was a helper,

C
I am, too.

C
I am a helper,

G7   C
See what I can do.

    (Act out a way of helping.)

Alternate verse: Substitute a child's name for the word "I" and change other words accordingly.

Shirley Scott
Orrville, OH

CHURCH, SUNDAY SCHOOL AND BIBLE SONGS

WE GO TO CHURCH

Sung to: "Mary Had a Little Lamb"

F
Happily we go to church,
C7   F
Go to church, go to church.
F
Happily we go to church
      C7   F
And sing this happy song.

F
Happily we greet our friends,
C7   F
Greet our friends, greet our friends.
F
Happily we greet our friends.
      C7   F
We're glad they came along.

Betty Ruth Baker
Waco, TX

GOOD MORNING

Sung to: "The Mulberry Bush"

C
Church is a place we meet our friends,
G7
Meet our friends, meet our friends.
C
Church is a place we meet our friends
     G7   C
And greet our friends, "Good Morning!"

Rachel Kramer
Beulah, ND

AT CHURCH

Sung to: "The Mulberry Bush"

C
This is the way we go to church,
   (Walk in a circle.)
G7
Go to church, go to church.
C
This is the way we go to church,
     G7   C
On happy Sunday morning.

C
This is the way we greet our friends,
   (Shake hands.)
G7
Greet our friends, greet our friends.
C
This is the way we greet our friends,
     G7   C
On happy Sunday morning.

C
This is the way we stand and sing,
   (Stand up straight.)
G7
Stand and sing, stand and sing.
C
This is the way we stand and sing,
     G7   C
On happy Sunday morning.

Additional verses: "This is the way we read the Bible; give our offerings; listen to our (pastor/minister/etc.); pray to God; wave goodbye." Have children make appropriate movements when singing each verse.

Betty Ruth Baker
Waco, TX

I'LL BE COMIN' RIGHT TO CHURCH

Sung to: "She'll Be Coming Round the Mountain"

F
I'll be comin' right to church when Sunday comes,

C7
I'll be comin' right to church when Sunday comes.

F
I'll be comin' right to church,

Bb
I'll be comin' right to church,

F   C7   F
I'll be comin' right to church when Sunday comes.

F
I'll be singin' songs of glory when I come,

C7
I'll be singin' songs of glory when I come.

F
I'll be singin' songs of glory,

Bb
I'll be singin' songs of glory,

F   C7   F
I'll be singin' songs of glory when I come.

F
I'll be sayin' lots of prayers when I come,

C7
I'll be sayin' lots of prayers when I come.

F
I'll be sayin' lots of prayers,

Bb
I'll be sayin' lots of prayers,

F   C7   F
I'll be sayin' lots of prayers when I come.

F
I'll be glad to talk to Jesus when I come,

C7
I'll be glad to talk to Jesus when I come.

F
I'll be glad to talk to Jesus,

Bb
I'll be glad to talk to Jesus,

F   C7   F
I'll be glad to talk to Jesus when I come.

Cindy Dingwall
Palatine, IL

OFF TO CHURCH WE GO

Sung to: "A-Hunting We Will Go"

F
Off to church we go,

F
Off to church we go.

F
We go happily to church,

C7   F
Because we love God so!

F
We talk to God each day,

F
We talk to God each day.

F
We tell God all sorts of things

C7   F
So He can guide our way!

Cindy Dingwall
Palatine, IL

EVERY SUNDAY

Sung to: "London Bridge"

F
Hand in hand we go to church,
   (Walk hand in hand.)

C7   F
Go to church, go to church.

F
Hand in hand we go to church,

C7   F
Every Sunday.

F
We sing praises to our Lord,
   (Imitate singers.)

C7   F
To our Lord, to our Lord.

F
We sing praises to our Lord,

C7   F
Every Sunday.

    F
We bow our heads and say our prayers,
   (Bow heads and fold hands.)

C7   F
Say our prayers, say our prayers.

    F
We bow our heads and say our prayers,

C7   F
Every Sunday.

Cindy Dingwall
Palatine, IL

GOING TO CHURCH

Sung to: "Michael, Row the Boat Ashore"

        C   F   C
Let us go to church right now, let us go,

        Em   Dm   G7 C
Let us go to church right now, let us go.

        C   F   C
Let us sing to praise the Lord, let us sing,

        Em   Dm   G7 C
Let us sing to praise the Lord, let us sing.

        C   F   C
Let us bow our heads in prayer, let us pray,

        Em   Dm   G7 C
Let us bow our heads in prayer, let us pray.

Additional verse: "Hear the (preacher/minister/etc.) talk of God, hear him preach."

Pamela Joyce Varner
Louisville, KY

COME TO CHURCH

Sung to: "Row, Row, Row Your Boat"

C
Come, come, come to church,

C
Come to sing and pray.

C
Talk to God, talk to God.

G7   C
Praise Him every day!

Cindy Dingwall
Palatine, IL

I LOVE YOU, LORD

Sung to: "Mary Had a Little Lamb"

F
(Child's name) went to church one day,
C7   F
Church one day, church one day.
F
(Child's name) went to church one day
      C7   F
To see (his/her) God and King.

F
(Child's name) knelt and prayed while there,
C7   F
Prayed while there, prayed while there.
F
(Child's name) knelt and prayed while there
C7   F
To (his/her) God and King.

F
(Child's name) said, "I love you, Lord,
C7   F
Love you, Lord; love you, Lord."
F
(Child's name) said, "I love you, Lord,"
      C7   F
Before (he/she) went to play.

Sr. Christine Yurick, VSC
Pittsburgh, PA

MY FRIENDS

Sung to: "Twinkle, Twinkle, Little Star"

C   F   C
In my church God always sends
F   C   G7   C
Boys and girls to be my friends.
C   F   C   G7
Some are short and some are tall,
C F   C   G7
But I always love them all.
C   F   C
In my church God always sends
F   C   G7   C
Boys and girls to be my friends.

Karen Vollmer
Wauseon, OH

WILL YOU BE A FRIEND OF MINE?

Sung to: "Mary Had a Little Lamb"

F
Will you be a friend of mine,
      C7   F
A friend of mine, a friend of mine?
F
Will you be a friend of mine
      C7   F
And come to church with me?

F
Will you sing a song with me,
      C7   F
A song with me, a song with me?
F
Will you sing a song with me
C7   F
At church today?

F
Will you say a prayer with me,
      C7   F
A prayer with me, a prayer with me?
F
Will you say a prayer with me
C7   F
At church today?

Karen Vollmer
Wauseon, OH

WE ALL GO TO CHURCH

Sung to: "Twinkle, Twinkle, Little Star"

C   F   C
We all go to church to pray
   F   C G7 C
And read the Bible every day.
C   F C G7
God is loving, we all know,
C   F C   G7
Love to others we should show.
C   F C
Tell your friends God really cares,
F C G7 C
And His love He always shares.

Joyce Raymond
Des Moines, IA

THE PEOPLE IN THE CHURCH

Sung to: "The Wheels on the Bus"

   F
The people in the church say lots of prayers,
 (Pretend to pray.)
C7   F
Lots of prayers, lots of prayers.
   F
The people in the church say lots of prayers,
C7   F
Every Sunday morning.

   F
The people in the choir sing lots of songs,
 (Imitate choir.)
C7   F
Lots of songs, lots of songs.
   F
The people in the choir sing lots of songs,
C7   F
Every Sunday morning.

   F
The children in the church wiggle and wiggle,
 (Wiggle.)
C7   F
Wiggle and wiggle, wiggle and wiggle.
   F
The children in the church wiggle and wiggle,
C7   F
Every Sunday morning.

Let children suggest ideas for other verses.

Cindy Dingwall
Palatine, IL

I LOVE TO GO TO CHURCH

Sung to: "I'm a Little Teapot"

 G   C G
I love to go to church to sing and pray,
  C G D7 G
To thank the Lord for each new day.
G   C G
When I go back home and start to play,
 C G D7 G
I use His teachings in every way!

Arlene Shapiro
Santa Ana, CA

I'M GLAD TO SEE YOU

Sung to: "Mary Had a Little Lamb"

F
(Child's name), I'm glad to see you,
C7   F
To see you, to see you.
F
(Child's name), I'm glad to see you
C7   F
At our church today.

Lanette L. Gutierrez
Olympia, WA

WE ARE GLAD TO SEE YOU

Sung to: "Frere Jacques"

F
Where is (child's name), where is (child's name)?
F
At church today, at church today.
F
We are glad to see you,
F
We are glad to see you.
F
Come and stay. Come and pray.

Karen Vollmer
Wauseon, OH

LOVE THE LORD

Sung to: "Row, Row, Row Your Boat"

C
Love, love, love the Lord,
C
Each and every day.
C
Cheerfully, cheerfully, cheerfully, cheerfully,
G   C
Follow in Christ's way.

C
March, march, march along,
C
Praising the Lord we love.
C
Singing our song, singing our song,
G   C
To our God above.

Susan M. Paprocki
Elmhurst, IL

SOMEPLACE SPECIAL

Sung to: "If You're Happy and You Know It"

F   C
I am going someplace special, my friend.
C   F
I am going someplace special, my friend.
Bb
I am going to (church/Sunday School).
F
I am going to (church/Sunday School).
C   F
I am going someplace special, my friend.

F   C
Will you go today with me, my friend?
C   F
Will you go today with me, my friend?
Bb
Will you go today with me?
F
We'll be happy as can be.
C   F
Will you go today with me, my friend?

Pamela Joyce Varner
Louisville, KY

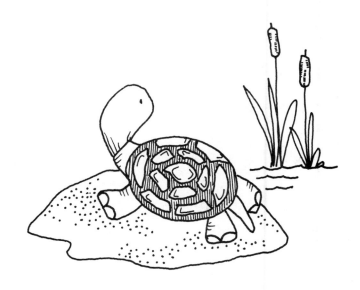

TO CHURCH SCHOOL

Sung to: "Did You Ever See a Lassie?"

F
I love to come to church school,
   C7   F
To church school, to church school.
F
I love to come to church school,
   C7   F
I see my friends here.
   C7   F
We sing and we pray,
   C7   F
We learn the Lord's way.
F
I love to come to church school,
   C7   F
I see my friends here.

Libby Wojasinski
Pasadena, TX

IN SUNDAY SCHOOL TODAY

Sung to: "The Mulberry Bush"

C
Wave your hand to greet the Lord,
G7
Greet the Lord, greet the Lord.
C
Wave your hand to greet the Lord,
   G7   C
In Sunday School today.

C
Clap your hands to praise the Lord,
G7
Praise the Lord, praise the Lord.
C
Clap your hands to praise the Lord,
   G7   C
In Sunday School today.

C
Fold your hands to pray to the Lord,
G7
Pray to the Lord, pray to the Lord.
C
Fold your hands to pray to the Lord,
   G7   C
In Sunday School today.

Additional verses: "Hop about to please the Lord; Throw a kiss to love the Lord."

Susan M. Paprocki
Elmhurst, IL

TO SUNDAY SCHOOL

Sung to: "A-Hunting We Will Go"

   F
To Sunday School we go,
   F
Our hearts are all aglow.
   F
With Jesus there we'll have no care,
   C   F
Because He loves us so.

   F
We learn to sing and pray
   F
And trust Him every day.
   F
He'll be our friend right to the end,
   C   F
In each and every way.

Judy Hall
Wytheville, VA

TO BIBLE SCHOOL

Sung to: "If You're Happy and You Know It"

C   G7
Oh, I really want to go to Bible School.

G7   C
Bible School is where I really want to be.

F
When to Bible School I go,

C
I will see my friends, I know,

G7   C
And I'll learn about how Jesus cares for me.

> **Sandy Chandler**
> **Owasso, OK**

THE KIDS COME MARCHING

Sung to: "When Johnny Comes Marching Home"

Em
The kids come marching one by one,

G
Hurrah! Hurrah!

Em
The kids come marching one by one,

G   B7
Hurrah! Hurrah!

Em   D7
The kids come marching one by one,

Em   B7
With lots of praise for the Holy One.

Em Am   Em   B7 Em
And they all come marching down

B7   Em
The aisle and through the church.

Additional verses: Substitute words such as these for "marching": "singing, praying, smiling."

> **Cindy Dingwall**
> **Palatine, IL**

LEARNING ABOUT GOD

Sung to: "Skip to My Lou"

C
(Child's name) comes to Sunday School,

G
(Child's name) comes to Sunday School,

C
(Child's name) comes to Sunday School

G   C
To learn about God and the Golden Rule.

Alternate verses: "(Child's name) comes to Bible School; (Child's name), (child's name) comes to school."

> **Jean L. Woods**
> **Tulsa, OK**

MARCHING, MARCHING

Sung to: "Sailing, Sailing"

C   F   C
Marching, marching, Jesus is our guide.

F   C
He shows us right and shows us wrong,

F   G
He's always by our side.

C   F   C
If we trust Him, He will lead the way.

F   C
It's very easy just to be

F   G   C
Good Christians every day.

> **Judy Hall**
> **Wytheville, VA**

CHRISTIAN SAILORS

Sung to: "The Marines' Hymn"

C   G7   C
Christian sailors for our Savior,

              G7   C
Christian sailors for our Lord,

                    G7   C
Come and sail our ship for Jesus,

               G7   C
Bring your Bible—climb aboard.

             F   C
Though at times the waters may be rough,

         F   C G7
God will guide us night and day.

       C   G7   C
He will always be our captain,

       C   G7   C
Follow Him—He is the way.

> **Judy Hall**
> **Wytheville, VA**

CHRISTIANS EVERYWHERE

Sung to: "The Caissons Go Rolling Along"

C
Marching here, marching there,

C
There are Christians everywhere,

Gdim   G7   C
Praising Jesus, the King of all kings.

C
Telling one, telling all,

C
"Come to Jesus, hear His call,"

Gdim   G7   C
Praising Jesus, the King of all kings.

             C
Give your heart to Him,

      F   C
He will free you from your sin.

Am   D7   G7
Then you'll have everlasting life.

   (Shout "Amen!")

                C   E7
'Cause wherever you go,

F   C
You will always know

Gdim   G7   C
Precious Jesus, the King of all kings.

> **Judy Hall**
> **Wytheville, VA**

GOOD SOLDIERS

Sung to: "Down by the Station"

D   A7   D
We are good soldiers, with the cross of Jesus,

   (Make cross with fingers.)

                     A7   D
Marching in His army each and every day.

   (March.)

                           A7   D
Come and join our army, marching for our Savior,

   (Point upward.)

               A7   D
Shouting "Amen!" on our way.

   (Stop and shout "Amen!")

> **Judy Hall**
> **Wytheville, VA**

DID YOU EVER SEE A CHRISTIAN?

Sung to: "Did You Ever See a Lassie?"

      F
Did you ever see a Christian,
  C7
A Christian, a Christian?
      F
Did you ever see a Christian
  C7   F
Go this way and that?
  C7   F
Go this way and that way,
  C7   F
Go this way and that way.
      F
Did you ever see a Christian
  C7   F
Go this way and that?

Additional verses: "Did you ever see a Christian pray this way
and that; sing this way and that?"

Cindy Dingwall
Palatine, IL

I AM A CHRISTIAN

Sung to: "You Are My Sunshine"

     F   Fdim   F
I am a Christian, a happy Christian,
 F7   Bb   F
I want to share my joy with you.
  F7   Bb   F
So if you follow in my footsteps,
     F   C7   F
You'll be a happy Christian, too.

         F   Fdim F
I walk the right path, oh, yes, the right path,
F7   Bb   F
As I follow in God's way.
   F7   Bb   F
We'll be so happy, so very happy,
         C7   F
Together on that path today.

Susan M. Paprocki
Elmhurst, IL

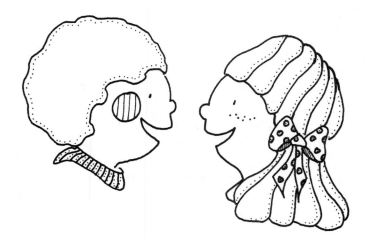

FOLLOW JESUS

Sung to: "Music, Music, Music"

F
I have now decided to
F
Follow Jesus Christ our Lord,
  G7   C7
I have now decided to follow
F   C7
Jesus Christ our Lord.

C7   F
I will follow him singing.
       C7
I will sing way down low
    C7
And way up high.
F   Cdim   Gm   C7
Let your voices fill the sky!

  F
I have now decided to
F
Follow Jesus Christ our Lord,
  G7   C7
I have now decided to follow
F   C7
Jesus Christ our Lord.

Kathy Smith
Milpitas, CA

TELL ALL THE PEOPLE

Sung to: "The Wheels on the Bus"

       F
Tell all the people Jesus is alive,
C7   F
Jesus is alive, Jesus is alive.
       F
Tell all the people Jesus is alive,
C7   F
All through the town.

         F
Be sure to spread God's love all around,
C7   F
Love all around, love all around.
         F
Be sure to spread God's love all around,
C7   F
All through the town.

F
Teach God's word all through your day,
C7   F
Through your day, through your day.
F
Teach God's word all through your day,
C7   F
All through the town.

F
Work and play with Jesus in mind,
C7   F
Jesus in mind, Jesus in mind.
F
Work and play with Jesus in mind,
C7   F
All through the town.

F
C'mon, children, let's praise the Lord,
C7   F
Praise the Lord, praise the Lord.
F
C'mon, children, let's praise the Lord,
C7   F
All through the town.

Susan M. Paprocki
Elmhurst, IL

78

JESUS IS OUR LORD

Sung to: "The Farmer in the Dell"

F
Jesus is our Lord,

F
Jesus is our Lord.

F
Hi-ho we're merry-oh,

F   C7   F
Jesus is our Lord.

F
The Lord chooses us,

F
The Lord chooses us.

F
Hi-ho we're merry-oh,

F   C7   F
The Lord chooses us.

F
We are called to serve,

F
We are called to serve.

F
Hi-ho we're merry-oh,

F   C7   F
We are called to serve.

F
To serve is to love,

F
To serve is to love.

F
Hi-ho we're merry-oh,

F   C7   F
To serve is to love.

Additional verses: "To love is to share; To share is to give; To give is to follow; We follow Christ."

Laura M. Koenig
New Milford, CT

GOD'S KINGDOM

Sung to: "She'll Be Coming Round the Mountain"

F
We're all part of His kingdom; yes, we are.

                                    C7
Oh, we're all part of His kingdom; yes, we are.

F
We are all part of His kingdom,

Bb
We are all part of His kingdom,

F   C7   F
We are all part of His kingdom; yes, we are.

F
We'll all stand up for Jesus; yes, we will.

(Stand.)

                                    C7
Oh, we'll all stand up for Jesus; yes, we will.

F
We will all stand up for Jesus,

Bb
We will all stand up for Jesus,

F   C7   F
We will all stand up for Jesus; yes, we will.

F
We'll all clap hands for Jesus; yes, we will.

(Clap.)

                                    C7
Oh, we'll all clap hands for Jesus; yes, we will.

F
We will all clap hands for Jesus,

Bb
We will all clap hands for Jesus,

F   C7   F
We will all clap hands for Jesus; yes, we will.

Additional verses: "We'll all turn around for Jesus; We'll all say 'Amen' for Jesus."

Shirley Scott
Orrville, OH

A SPECIAL BOOK

Sung to: "The Mulberry Bush"

C
The Bible is a special book,
G7
Special book, special book.
C
The Bible is a special book
G7   C
My teacher reads to me.

C
It tells of people long ago,
G7
Long ago, long ago.
C
It tells of people long ago
G7   C
And God's great love for me.

C
It tells us how He made the world,
G7
Made the world, made the world.
C
It tells us how He made the world,
G7   C
The dry land and the sea.

C
It tells us how He sent His Son,
G7
Sent His Son, sent His Son.
C
It tells us how He sent His Son
G7   C
And how His Son loves me.

Libby Wojasinski
Pasadena, TX

THE BIBLE IS ITS NAME

Sung to: "Bingo"

        F   Bb   F
There is a book that tells it all,
        F   C7   F
The Bible is its name-o.
F   Bb   C7   F   F   Bb
B-I-B-L-E, B-I-B-L-E, B-I-B-L-E,
            C7   F
The Bible is its name-o.

        F   Bb   F
Read stories from the Old or New,
        F   C7   F
The Bible is its name-o.
F   Bb   C7   F   F   Bb
B-I-B-L-E, B-I-B-L-E, B-I-B-L-E,
            C7   F
The Bible is its name-o.

F   Bb   F
Give me the Book, God's Holy Word,
        F   C7   F
The Bible is its name-o.
F   Bb   C7   F   F   Bb
B-I-B-L-E, B-I-B-L-E, B-I-B-L-E,
            C7   F
The Bible is its name-o.

Judy Hall
Wytheville, VA

80

GOD'S HOLY WORD

Sung to: "Did You Ever See a Lassie?"

       F
Did you ever see a Bible,

  C   F
A Bible, a Bible?

       F
Did you ever see a Bible?

  C   F
It's God's Holy Word.

  C   F
I open the pages

  C   F
To stories I've heard.

    F
Yes, this is the Bible,

  C   F
It's God's Holy Word.

Lois Poppe
Lincoln, NE

MY FAVORITE BOOK

Sung to: "My Bonnie Lies Over the Ocean"

  C   F   C
My favorite book is the Bible,

  C   D7   G
It tells me that Jesus loves me.

  C   F   C
My favorite book is the Bible,

   F   G   C
Just open its pages and see.

C   F
God's Word, God's Word,

  G   C
The Bible is precious to me, to me.

C   F
God's Word, God's Word,

  G   C
The Bible is precious to me.

Barbara Dunn
Hollidaysburg, PA

THIS I KNOW

Sung to: "Jingle Bells"

C
Long ago, this I know,

C
The Bible tells it all.

F   C
Jesus spoke to gatherings,

  D7   G7
He talked to one and all.

C
"Follow me, you will see

   C
I am the only way."

F   C
Give your heart to Jesus —

  G7   C
Be a Christian every day. Yay!

Judy Hall
Wytheville, VA

THE BIBLE

Sung to: "The Farmer in the Dell"

      C
The Bible is God's Word,

      C
The Bible is God's Word

      C
To read and study every day.

      G   C
The Bible is God's Word.

Barbara Dunn
Hollidaysburg, PA

READ THE BOOK

Sung to: "Row, Row, Row Your Boat"

C
Read, read, read The Book,
C
Read it every day.
C
Learn about the gifts of life
    G   C
And all about God's way.

C
Say, say, say your prayers,
C
Say them every day.
C
Talk to God — He answers prayers.
    G   C
He'll help in every way.

Judy Hall
Wytheville, VA

B-I-B-L-E

Sung to: "Old MacDonald Had a Farm"

C   F   C   C G C
There's a book that you should read, B-I-B-L-E.
C   F   C   C G C
There you'll find the facts you need, B-I-B-L-E.
C
How to live, how to grow,
C
All about people long ago.
C   F   C   C G C
There's a book that you should read, B-I-B-L-E.

Debra Lindahl
Libertyville, IL

IN THE BIBLE

Sung to: "Oh, My Darling Clementine"

            C
In the Bible, there are stories
              G
All about His precious love,
                   C
'Bout how God so loved the world,
  G   C
He sent His Son from up above.

           C
If we trust Him and believe Him,
              G
He will save us all from sin.
            C
We will all have life eternal,
      G   C
And our new life will begin.

Judy Hall
Wytheville, VA

82

PRAYER, PRAISE
AND
THANK-YOU SONGS

BE A CHRISTIAN

Sung to: "If You're Happy and You Know It"

F   C
Put your arm around a friend, round a friend.

   (Put arm around neighbor.)

          C   F
Put your arm around a friend, round a friend.

        Bb
Put your arm around a friend,

   F
Be a Christian to the end.

          C   F
Put your arm around a friend, round a friend.

         F   C
Now get on your knees and pray to the Lord.

    (Kneel.)

          C   F
Now get on your knees and pray to the Lord.

        Bb
Now get on your knees and pray,

   F
Be a Christian every day.

          C   F
Now get on your knees and pray to the Lord.

         F   C
Raise your hands and shout "Amen," shout "Amen!"

    (Raise hands and shout.)

          C   F
Raise your hands and shout "Amen," shout "Amen!"

        Bb
Raise your hands and shout "Amen!"

   F
Singing praises to the end.

          C   F
Raise your hands and shout "Amen," shout "Amen!"

                        Judy Hall
                        Wytheville, VA

I'M A LITTLE CHRISTIAN

Sung to: "I'm a Little Teapot"

G
I'm a little Christian,

   C   G
I like to say my prayers,

C   G   D7   G
Thanking the Lord who always cares.

G
If you ever need Him,

C   G
He'll be there,

   C   G   D7   G
So just remember to say a prayer.

                        Tina Kinsley
                        York, PA

GETTING READY TO PRAY

Sung to: "London Bridge"

F
Jesus wants us to pray now,

C7   F
To pray now, to pray now.

F
Jesus wants us to pray now.

C7   F
Let's bow our heads.

F
Jesus wants us to pray now,

C7   F
To pray now, to pray now.

F
Jesus wants us to pray now.

C7   F
Let's fold our hands.

F
Jesus wants us to pray now,

C7   F
To pray now, to pray now.

F
Jesus wants us to pray now.

C7   F
Let's be quiet.

                        Mary K. Miller
                        Greenville, PA

DO YOU KNOW WHO JESUS IS?

Sung to: "The Muffin Man"

G
Do you know who Jesus is,
C   D7
Who Jesus is, who Jesus is?
G
Do you know who Jesus is?
   D7   G
I'll tell you who He is.

G
Jesus is God's only Son,
C   D7
God's only Son, God's only Son.
G
Jesus is God's only Son.
   D7   G
He came for everyone.

G
Jesus likes to hear us pray,
C   D7
Hear us pray, hear us pray.
G
Jesus likes to hear us pray,
   D7   G
So talk to Him each day.

Cindy Dingwall
Palatine, IL

STAND UP TALL

Sung to: "Row, Row, Row Your Boat"

F
Clap, clap, clap your hands,
F
Stand up tall for Jesus.
F
Bow your head, fold your hands.
C7   F
Say a prayer to thank Him.

Let children take turns telling what they are thankful for.

Marlene V. Filsinger
Snyder, NY

MY TRUE FRIEND

Sung to: "I'm a Little Teapot"

G
Jesus is my true friend,
C   G
Yes, I know.
C   G   D7   G
He helps me while I grow.
G
When I want to thank Him,
C   G
I just pray,
          C   D7   G
"I love you in a great big way."

Marlene V. Filsinger
Snyder, NY

LET'S TALK TO JESUS

Sung to: "Mary Had a Little Lamb"

F
Close your eyes and bow your head,
C7   F
Bow your head, bow your head.
F
Close your eyes and bow your head.
   C7   F
Let's talk to Jesus now.

Rachel Kramer
Beulah, ND

85

HOLY IS HIS NAME

Sung to: "Old MacDonald Had a Farm"

F   Bb   F
Jesus Christ is King of kings,
F   C   F
Holy is His name.
F   Bb   F
And in Him we do all things,
F   C   F
Holy is His name.

        F
With a praise, praise here,
        F
And a praise, praise there,
F
Here a praise, there a praise,
F
Everywhere a praise, praise.
         Bb   F
Jesus Christ is King of kings,
F   C   F
Holy is His name.

F   Bb   F
Jesus Christ is Lord of lords,
F   C   F
Holy is His name.
F   Bb   F
From beginning to the end,
F   C   F
He remains the same.

        F
With a glory, glory here,
        F
And a glory, glory there,
F
Here a glory, there a glory,
F
Everywhere a glory, glory.
F   Bb   F
Jesus Christ is King of kings,
F   C   F
Holy is His name.

F   Bb   F
Jesus Christ is Savior dear,
F   C   F
Holy is His name.
F   Bb   F
And with Him we know no fear,
F   C   F
Holy is His name.

        F
With an alleluia here,
        F
And an alleluia there,
F
Here an alle-, there an alle-,
F
Everywhere an alleluia.
F   Bb   F
Jesus Christ is King of kings,
F   C   F
Holy is His name.

Laura M. Koenig
New Milford, CT

WHO'S OUR SAVIOR?

Sung to: "Old MacDonald Had a Farm"

F   Bb   F   F   C   F
Who's our Savior—what's His name? J-E-S-U-S.
F   Bb   F   F   C   F
Who above the earth shall reign? J-E-S-U-S.

        F
With a praise Him here,
        F
And a praise Him there,
F
Praise Him, praise Him,
F
Everybody praise Him!
F   Bb   F   F   C   F
Praise our Savior—what's His name? J-E-S-U-S.

Nancy L. Riley
Loveland, CO

PRAISE JESUS

Sung to: "London Bridge"

F
Praise Jesus every day,
C7   F
Every day, every day.
F
Praise Jesus every day,
C7   F
And you'll be happy.

F
Pray to Jesus every day,
C7   F
Every day, every day.
F
Pray to Jesus every day,
C7   F
And you'll be happy.

F
Tell your friends about His life,
C7   F
About His life, about His life.
F
Tell your friends about His life,
C7   F
And they'll be happy.

F
Tell your friends about His love,
C7   F
About His love, about His love.
F
Tell your friends about His love,
   C7   F
And they'll be happy.

Cathy Jacobson
Winthrop, WA

YOU WILL BE BLESSED

Sung to: "The Mulberry Bush"

C
Praise Jesus all day long,
   (Raise hands in the air.)
G7
All day long, all day long.
C
Praise Jesus all day long,
G7   C
And you will be blessed.

C
Love your family all day long,
   (Cross arms over chest.)
G7
All day long, all day long.
C
Love your family all day long,
G7   C
And you will be blessed.

C
Pray to Jesus all day long,
   (Fold hands in prayer.)
G7
All day long, all day long.
C
Pray to Jesus all day long,
G7   C
And you will be blessed.

Mandy Bortz
Chappaqua, NY

TALKED TO JESUS

Sung to: "Found a Peanut"

F
Talked to Jesus, talked to Jesus,

                C7
Talked to Jesus last night.

               F
Last night I talked to Jesus,

      C7   F
Talked to Jesus last night.

F
Praised the Lord, praised the Lord,

              C7
Praised the Lord last night.

            F
Last night I praised the Lord,

     C7   F
Praised the Lord last night.

F
Thanked the Lord, thanked the Lord,

            C7
Thanked the Lord last night.

           F
Last night I thanked the Lord,

     C7   F
Thanked the Lord last night.

The words "yesterday" and "today" can be substituted for "last night." Let children suggest ideas for other verses.

Cindy Dingwall
Palatine, IL

GOD SO LOVED THE WORLD

Sung to: "The Farmer in the Dell"

   F
For God so loved the world

   F
He gave His only Son

    F
That whosoever believes in Him

       C   F
Has everlasting life.

Florence Dieckmann
Roanoke, VA

TAKE ME OUT TO SEE JESUS

Sung to: "Take Me Out to the Ball Game"

C   G
Take me out to see Jesus,

C   G
Take me out to the crowd.

A7   Dm
I want to thank Him for what He's done,

D7   G7
In my life, He's Number One!

          C   G
Oh, it's shout out loud for Jesus!

     C7   F
He loves us more than you know.

         F   F#dim C
For it's one—two—three shouts "Hurray!"

      Dm G   C
To Jerusalem we go!

Emily Lilly
Pompano Beach, FL

THANKSGIVING DAY

Sung to: "Hush, Little Baby"

F   C7
Thanking Him for birds that sing,

             F
Thanking Him, our special King.

F   C7
Thanking God for everything,

           F
On Thanksgiving Day.

F   C7
Giving thanks to the Holy One

           F
For sending us His only Son.

            C7
We thank Him for all He's done,

           F
On Thanksgiving Day.

Judy Hall
Wytheville, VA

GIVE THANKS

Sung to: "Oh, My Darling Clementine"

F
Oh, give thanks; oh, give thanks
    F   C7
To the Father up above.

                  F
Sent His Son to be our Savior,
    C7   F
Gave the world His lasting love.

   F
If we trust Him, if we trust Him,
            C7
He will live within our hearts.
          F
He will give us life eternal,
    C7   F
And from us He'll never part.

Judy Hall
Wytheville, VA

THANKS BE TO JESUS

Sung to: "Skip to My Lou"

F
Thanks be to Jesus for all good things,
C7
Thanks be to Jesus for all good things,
F
Thanks be to Jesus for all good things.
C7   F
Thank you, God, for everything.

F
Thanks for my family and all their love,
C7
Thanks for my family and all their love,
F
Thanks for my family and all their love.
C7   F
Thank you, God, for everything.

Let children suggest ideas for other verses.

Cindy Dingwall
Palatine, IL

THANK YOU, JESUS

Sung to: "London Bridge"

F
Thank you, Jesus, for our food,
C7   F
For our food, for our food.
F
Thank you, Jesus, for our food.
C7   F
Thank you, Jesus.

F
Thank you, Jesus, for our friends,
C7   F
For our friends, for our friends.
F
Thank you, Jesus, for our friends.
C7   F
Thank you, Jesus.

F
Thank you, Jesus, for our families,
C7   F
For our families, for our families.
F
Thank you, Jesus, for our families.
C7   F
Thank you, Jesus.

Additional verses: "Thank you, Jesus, for our toys; for our pets; for our church."

Sue Brown
Louisville, KY

89

LOVE FOR EVERYONE

Sung to: "Three Blind Mice"

<pre>
C   G   C   C   G   C
Love, love, love; love, love, love,
C   G   C   C   G   C
Sent from above, sent from above.
C   G   C
Jesus lived and died for me,
            G   C
That's how God said it would be.
C   G   C
Love for everyone to see,
C   G   C
Love, love, love.
</pre>

Janet Harris
Annandale, NJ

YOU'RE MY FRIEND FOREVER

Sung to: "Skip to My Lou"

Chorus:

<pre>
F
Thank you, Jesus, for what you do,
C7
Thank you, Jesus, for what you do,
F
Thank you, Jesus, for what you do.
C7   F
You're my friend forever.

F
Food and clothes and family, too,
C7
Flowers, trees and sky so blue,
F
Gifts of God, they're all from you.
C7   F
You're my friend forever.
</pre>

Chorus

Judy Hall
Wytheville, VA

LET'S CLAP OUR HANDS

Sung to: "The Mulberry Bush"

<pre>
C
Jesus loves you and me,
G7
You and me, you and me.
C
Jesus loves you and me,
  G7   C
So let's all clap our hands!

C
Jesus died for you and me,
G7
You and me, you and me.
C
Jesus died for you and me,
  G7   C
So let's all clap our hands!

C
Jesus rose for you and me,
G7
You and me, you and me.
C
Jesus rose for you and me,
  G7   C
So let's all clap our hands!

C
Jesus lives for you and me,
G7
You and me, you and me.
C
Jesus lives for you and me,
  G7   C
So let's all clap our hands!
</pre>

Kathy Sizer
Tustin, CA

GOD SO LOVED US

Sung to: "Frere Jacques"

C
God so loved us, God so loved us,

C
You and me, you and me,

C
He gave us His Son, Jesus.

C
In our hearts He frees us

C
Instantly, instantly!

C
He's my Savior, He's my Savior,

C
This I know, this I know.

C
Never will He leave me.

C
In my heart He will be

C
Constantly, constantly!

Marie Wheeler
Tacoma, WA

HE SENT HIS ONLY SON

Sung to: "Twinkle, Twinkle, Little Star"

C   F   C
God loves each and every one,

F   C   G7   C
That is why He sent His Son.

C   F   C   G7
Saving us from every sin,

C   F   C   G7
He has come to live within.

C   F   C
God loves each and every one,

F   C   G7   C
That is why He sent His Son.

Judy Hall
Wytheville, VA

OH, I LOVE GOD!

Sung to: "Oh, Susanna"

D
I come to church each Sunday

                  A7
With my heart bursting with love.

D
Oh, I come to church each Sunday

        A7   D
With my heart bursting with love.

Chorus:

G
Oh, I love God!

D   A7
He sent His only Son.

D
He gave this very special gift

       A7   D
For each and every one.

D
I know God gave us Jesus,

          A7
His one and only Son.

D
Jesus came into this world

    A7   D
And died for everyone.

Chorus

Cindy Dingwall
Palatine, IL

HE IS THE ONE

Sung to: "When the Saints Go Marching In"

       D
He is the one, the only one,
                 A7
Who gave His life for you and me.
         D   G
Open up your hearts for Jesus,
       D   A7   D
And the truth will set you free.

          D
Go tell your friends, all of your friends,
                 A7
He gave His life for you and me.
      D   G
Let them give their hearts to Jesus.
      D   A7   D
Oh, so happy they will be!

Judy Hall
Wytheville, VA

JESUS, JESUS

Sung to: "Camptown Races"

C
Who walked on the sea so blue?
G
Jesus, Jesus.
C
Died for me and died for you?
G   C
Jesus Christ the Lord.
C
Give to Him your heart,
     F   C
From you He'll never part.
C
Trust in Him, a friend so true,
G   C
Jesus Christ the Lord.

Judy Hall
Wytheville, VA

MY SAVIOR

Sung to: "London Bridge"

C
Jesus helps me to forgive,
G   C
To forgive, to forgive.
C
Jesus helps me to forgive.
G   C
Jesus is my Savior.

C
Jesus helps me love my friends,
G   C
Love my friends, love my friends.
C
Jesus helps me love my friends.
G   C
Jesus is my Savior.

Additional verse: "Jesus died to set me free."

Patricia Bortz
Chappaqua, NY

JESUS CHRIST IS MY LORD

Sung to: "Mary Had a Little Lamb"

F
Jesus Christ is my Lord,
C7   F
Is my Lord, is my Lord.
F
Jesus Christ is my Lord,
       C7   F
And He takes care of me.

       F
I know that He loves me,
C7   F
Loves me, loves me.
      F
I know that He loves me,
     C7   F
Because He died for me.

Christopher Steinfeld
Pine Island, NY

TITLE INDEX

TITLE INDEX

Activity Books

BEST OF TOTLINE® SERIES
Totline Magazine's best ideas.
Best of Totline
Best of Totline Parent Flyers

BUSY BEES SERIES
Seasonal ideas for twos and threes.
Busy Bees—Fall
Busy Bees—Winter
Busy Bees—Spring
Busy Bees—Summer

CELEBRATION SERIES
Early learning through celebrations.
Small World Celebrations
Special Day Celebrations
Great Big Holiday Celebrations
Celebrating Likes and Differences

EXPLORING SERIES
Versatile, hands-on learning.
Exploring Sand
Exploring Water
Exploring Wood

FOUR SEASONS
Active learning through the year.
Four Seasons—Art
Four Seasons—Math
Four Seasons—Movement
Four Seasons—Science

GREAT BIG THEMES SERIES
Giant units designed around a theme.
Space • Zoo • Circus

LEARNING & CARING ABOUT
Teach children about their world.
Our World
Our Town

PIGGYBACK® SONGS
New songs sung to the tunes of childhood favorites!
Piggyback Songs
More Piggyback Songs
Piggyback Songs for Infants and Toddlers
Holiday Piggyback Songs
Animal Piggyback Songs
Piggyback Songs for School
Piggyback Songs to Sign
Spanish Piggyback Songs
More Piggyback Songs for School

PLAY & LEARN SERIES
Learning through familiar objects.
Play & Learn with Magnets
Play & Learn with Rubber Stamps
Play & Learn with Photos
Play & Learn with Stickers
Play & Learn with Paper Shapes & Borders

1•2•3 SERIES
Open-ended learning.
1•2•3 Art
1•2•3 Games
1•2•3 Colors
1•2•3 Puppets
1•2•3 Reading & Writing
1•2•3 Rhymes, Stories & Songs
1•2•3 Math
1•2•3 Science
1•2•3 Shapes

THEME-A-SAURUS® SERIES
Classroom-tested, instant themes.
Theme-A-Saurus
Theme-A-Saurus II
Toddler Theme-A-Saurus
Alphabet Theme-A-Saurus
Nursery Rhyme Theme-A-Saurus
Storytime Theme-A-Saurus
Multisensory Theme-A-Saurus

Parent Books

A YEAR OF FUN SERIES
Age-specific books for parenting.
Just for Babies • Just for Ones
Just for Twos • Just for Threes
Just for Fours • Just for Fives

BEGINNING FUN WITH ART
Introduce your child to art fun.
Craft Sticks • Crayons • Felt
Glue • Paint • Paper Shapes
Modeling Dough • Tissue Paper
Scissors • Rubber Stamps
Stickers • Yarn

BEGINNING FUN WITH SCIENCE
Spark your child's interest in science.
Bugs & Butterflies • Plants & Flowers • Magnets • Rainbows & Colors • Sand & Shells • Water & Bubbles

LEARNING EVERYWHERE
Discover teaching opportunities everywhere you go.
Teaching House • Teaching Trips
Teaching Town

Story Time
Delightful stories with related activity ideas, snacks, and songs.

KIDS CELEBRATE SERIES
Kids Celebrate the Alphabet
Kids Celebrate Numbers

HUFF AND PUFF® SERIES
Huff and Puff's Snowy Day
Huff and Puff on Groundhog Day
Huff and Puff's Hat Relay
Huff and Puff's April Showers
Huff and Puff's Hawaiian Rainbow
Huff and Puff Go to Camp
Huff and Puff's Fourth of July
Huff and Puff Around the World
Huff and Puff Go to School
Huff and Puff on Halloween
Huff and Puff on Thanksgiving
Huff and Puff's Foggy Christmas

NATURE SERIES
The Bear and the Mountain
Ellie the Evergreen
The Wishing Fish

Resources

BEAR HUGS® SERIES
Encourage positive attitudes.
Remembering the Rules
Staying in Line
Circle Time
Transition Times
Time Out
Saying Goodbye
Meals and Snacks
Nap Time
Cleanup
Fostering Self-Esteem
Being Afraid
Saving the Earth
Being Responsible
Getting Along
Being Healthy
Welcoming Children
Respecting Others
Accepting Change

MIX & MATCH PATTERNS
Simple patterns to save time!
Animal • Everyday
Holiday • Nature

PROBLEM SOLVING SAFARI
Teaching problem solving skills.
Problem Solving—Art
Problem Solving—Blocks
Problem Solving—Dramatic Play
Problem Solving—Manipulatives
Problem Solving—Outdoors
Problem Solving—Science

101 TIPS FOR DIRECTORS
Valuable tips for busy directors.
Staff and Parent Self-Esteem
Parent Communication
Health and Safety
Marketing Your Center
Resources for You and Your Center
Child Development Training

101 TIPS FOR PRESCHOOL TEACHERS
Creating Theme Environments
Encouraging Creativity
Developing Motor Skills
Developing Language Skills
Teaching Basic Concepts
Spicing Up Learning Centers

101 TIPS FOR TODDLER TEACHERS
Classroom Management
Discovery Play
Dramatic Play
Large Motor Play
Small Motor Play
Word Play

1001 SERIES
Super reference books.
1001 Teaching Props
1001 Teaching Tips
1001 Rhymes & Fingerplays

SNACKS SERIES
Nutrition combines with learning.
Super Snacks
Healthy Snacks
Teaching Snacks
Multicultural Snacks

Puzzles & Posters

PUZZLES
Kids Celebrate the Alphabet
Kids Celebrate Numbers
African Adventure
Underwater Adventure
Bear Hugs Health Puzzles
Busy Bees

POSTERS
We Work and Play Together
Bear Hugs Sing-Along Health Posters
Busy Bees Area Posters

If you like Totline® Books,
You'll love Totline® Magazine!

For fresh ideas that challenge and engage young children in active learning, reach for **Totline® Magazine**—Proven ideas from innovative teachers!

FREE full-color poster in each issue!

Each issue includes

- Seasonal learning themes
- Stories, songs, and rhymes
- Open-ended art projects
- Science explorations
- Reproducible parent pages
- Ready-made teaching materials
- Activities just for toddlers
- Reproducible healthy snack recipes